Rebalancing the social and economic

Rebalancing the social and economic

Learning, partnership and place

Edited by
Chris Duke
Mike Osborne
and Bruce Wilson

promoting adult learning

© 2005 National Institute of Adult Continuing Education
(England and Wales)

21 De Montfort Street
Leicester
LE1 7GE

Company registration no. 2603322
Charity registration no. 1002775

NIACE has a broad remit to promote lifelong learning opportunities for adults.
NIACE works to develop increased participation in education and training,
particularly for those who do not have easy access because of class, gender,
age, race, language and culture, learning difficulties or disabilities,
or insufficient financial resources.

You can find NIACE online at www.niace.org.uk

Cataloguing in Publication Data
A CIP record of this title is available from the British Library

Designed and typeset by Avon DataSet Ltd, Bidford-on-Avon, Warwickshire
Printed and bound in the UK by Latimer Trend & Company Ltd, Plymouth

ISBN: 1 86201 270 9

Contents

Chapter 1

Beyond the economic: finding balanced development in a global environment

Chris Duke*, Mike Osborne**, Bruce Wilson***
**Director (Higher Education) NIACE UK, Professor of Regional Learning
and Partnerships, School of Social Science and Planning, RMIT
University, Australia;
**Professor of Lifelong Education and Head of the Division of
Academic Innovation and Continuing Education, University
of Stirling, Scotland;
***Professor of Organisation and Work Design and Head of the School
of Social Science and Planning, RMIT University, Austrailia*

Looking at social priorities

Over the past decade, governments throughout all parts of the world have been preoccupied with issues related to the global economy and its implications for international relations. In this context many governments have given priority to policies that promote enhanced international competitiveness for businesses, and restrain the role of the public sector, while protecting national interests. At the same time they have been subject to rising expectations with respect to demands for improved infrastructure for health, education and other community services. These demands have intensified as the emerging patterns of global economic activity have led to increasing differentiation in the circumstances of communities, and particularly, in many countries, between metropolitan and more rural regional communities.

These developments and unintended consequences throw into some perspective the role of national government policies to support and develop 'social capital' initiatives in communities. Historically many governments have tended to view society as a single entity, where general policies for education, health and social development can be promulgated for the whole nation. More recently, governments have come to see the need for more local solutions, both to engage local energies more effectively and to acknowledge and respond to the diversity of settings and needs. There still remains however a substantial body of evidence pointing to the need for more sustained and effective devolved policy development and decision-making.

Linked to these developments, many people have increasingly come to identify with their local community, seeing local relationships as an important foundation for economic, social and cultural action. This is not a new phenomenon, but community-based initiatives and connections have become a critical site for the expression of people's needs and aspirations, and for the practical development of economic, educational, cultural and environmental projects. Conversely, once discredited, 'community engagement' has been of increasing interest to governments as a means of both refining and delivering social policy initiatives.

The interaction of these trends has meant that governments are showing growing interest in interventions targeted at communities and regions. Social inclusion is an emerging policy imperative alongside competitive economic development. In some cases the interventions have relied on the development or renewal of physical infrastructure, such as hospitals and public transport systems. Increasingly however, the interventions have addressed challenges associated with locally-based social infrastructure and relationships, often articulated in terms of 'community building', enhancing 'social capital' or developing 'learning communities and regions'. Others have aimed at linking economic initiatives directly with social objectives. Partnerships have been an important mechanism for these interventions, involving various mixes of public sector, private and commercial interests, and community-based, non-profit organisations, the ever more frequently-cited third sector.

The scale and importance of these interventions raise significant questions about policy and programme development: what kinds of interventions work most effectively in achieving which goals? What are the implications of different kinds of partnerships for the effectiveness of various interventions? Are different kinds of interventions more appropriate for influencing some social or economic objectives rather than others? What lessons can be learned about the effectiveness of initiatives that combine both economic and social objectives? These questions have been at the centre of discussions within the European domain concerning the development of the *lifelong learning region* and the recent R3L Initiative (European Commission, 2002), and are pertinent elsewhere.

The range of concepts that might be applied is itself problematic. For example the concept of *social capital* may be seen as quite restricted if it concentrates on issues of social cohesiveness and the associated ideas of *community* and general well-being, rather than on the structural dimensions of social and economic life which drive not only the approach to economic development, but also the underlying processes which produce inequality. Other broad concepts, such as *sustainability*, are hard to define precisely, particularly when they have become debased through excessive and inappropriate use.

Community can be a frail notion and a fragile flower: community-building may not be a process that can be implemented as fiat by government. It requires careful engagement with key stakeholders and a commitment to clear and accepted ground rules for participation and for 'belonging'. This goes beyond a broad willingness to let people have their say. It means providing clear frameworks for decision-making, for resource allocation, and for exploring and consolidating relationships that have substance, openness and transparency.

Concepts associated with *learning economies* and *societies* are not new. Relatively new, however, is the acknowledgment of a link between lifelong learning and social-physical infrastructure. In developing national and regional policies for investment, governments are considering more integrated approaches, with the public provision of education facilities, transport, housing, communications, health care, and a role for an enlightened private sector which may invest significantly more than the public sector, if the investment climate created by governments is encouraging. It is important to discover what forms of partnership, linkage and co-investment work best in which circumstances and are most effective at engaging with and enhancing constructive social outcomes.

There are also many interpretations of the linked concept of the *learning city, region or city-region*, and these draw upon a range of literatures including those concerned with innovation, entrepreneurship and knowledge capture (see Sankey and Osborne, 2005). Again the concept is not new, but with the explicit addition of a 'lifelong' dimension, a re-invigoration of what has been a rather slippery notion seems to be occurring. Partnership and the mobilising of stakeholders from the public and private sectors to support lifelong learning have become key in the drive towards local and regional regeneration.

Pascal: the story so far

The Pascal Observatory was established jointly by RMIT and Stirling Universities in partnership with regional governments in Victoria and the United Kingdom, following an OECD Conference on Learning Regions conducted in Melbourne in October 2002. Pascal is an international observatory – a strategic information tracking and sharing service on Place Management, Social Capital and Learning Regions in what is often called the 'New Economy'. It aspires to support sustainable development based in experience and evidence of what works. Its central purpose, as set out in the original brochure, is:

> to enable effective delivery of policies that improve the quality of living and working circumstances at local and regional levels, recognising the importance of learning, social capital and the necessity of partnership for the successful implementation of policy. (Pascal, 2003)

It focuses especially on regional initiatives that explicitly embrace learning to develop a systematic planning framework that seeks to encompass multiple perspectives – administrative, cultural, geographical, physical and political. It involves looking at life from the perspective of people and places, rather than as separate programmes delivered for them. Other partners from Europe and North America are in the process of joining Pascal, extending the collaboration between researchers and policy-makers to a wider international environment.

The Observatory is itself an example of an innovative partnership supporting community engagement. It has supported and generated a number of initiatives addressing various aspects of partnership designed to foster community building, social capital and citizenship. These projects encompass issues relating to the measurement of social capital, urban regeneration, learning and innovation in urban networks, schooling and social capital, informal and formal networks, community strengthening, and the implications of different kinds of public/private partnerships.

Pascal's central concern is to support policy-makers who believe that *the social* should be at the heart of public policy, in balance with, and encompassing, the economic agenda. It is important that they understand *the economic* as a means for achieving social objectives, rather than social issues being addressed in order only to improve economic performance.

In June 2005 the first woman vice-chancellor of the University of Cambridge wrote what appears to have been the first ever letter, in 800 years, to all the University's alumni. Here she indicated a need 'to engage all of you far more closely in the future' if Cambridge was to meet the challenges ahead. In this letter Professor Alison Richard conveys 'my first message to the new Government' (the Blair Administration on entering its 3rd term): '"Great economies need great universities", it is said; "Great *societies* need great universities", I reply'.

Pascal is inescapably political – it is concerned with assumptions behind the exercise of power and political authority. It is also civic – concerned with the way that citizens live, and are enabled to live more fully and confidently, in their place of life and work – the *civis*. Recognition of the abiding importance of place to people and to the management of their lives and circumstances – and of the need to bring different resources and specialised services together for this purpose – led to the creation, mainly it seems in Australia, of the term *place management* (PM). This had an initially puzzled reception in Europe. Within the short lifespan of the Observatory the term has become less unfamiliar and sits well enough alongside Pascal's two other key points of reference: *social capital* (SC); and the *learning city, region or city-region* (LCR).

At first Pascal was marked by almost anguished rumination about the relationship and priority between these three points on its triangle of activity – PM, SC, and LCR. Wrapping around them is the older and no less diffuse concept of lifelong learning; without this the interest of several early partners and contributors, including encouragement and informal intellectual support from some in the education wing of OECD, would have been slight.

As the glass cleared it became evident that it was not so much these three separate points, but the connection between them and the space marked out by linking the points in the triangle, that was interesting and important. There was no need for weighting and prioritising to say which mattered more. The more interesting and important issues proved to be: whether and how they connect up; what kinds of planning, activities and relationships are found in the shared space; and how the plethora of different public, private and third-sector 'stakeholders' cooperate or compete within this arena.

The salience throughout of *lifelong learning* manifests itself in the centrality of learning and the quest to make activity - policy-making, implementation and evaluation - more *'learning-ful'*. How do the stakeholders in the private, public and third sectors, with their different special interests, expertise and responsibilities, and their different forms of organisation, learn from their own experience? As with individuals, the surest sign that learning has occurred is changed behaviour and, behind that, different understanding. Along with this goes partnership – how to cooperate to achieve complex outcomes involving many parties having different histories, capabilities and priorities?

It became evident that a central challenge was another form of partnership and mutual learning: that between policy-makers and their executive arms on the one hand, and the scholars and scholarship of – mainly – the universities on the other. Pascal must guard assiduously against the benevolent and unintentional but pervasive tendency of scholars with their persuasive, fascinating discourse simply to take over, elbowing aside those who have to *do* as well as think and talk.

Here is an innocent cultural imperialism somewhat resembling the way that the middle classes naturally colonise and capture services intended for the poor. However, the analogy is dangerous, if it implies inferior intellectual capability and resources – other than perhaps time for reflection and conferring – on the part of those who *do*. Pascal not only critically examines partnership. It also seeks to model it and practise it, holding the ring for constructive discourse between those in the policy arena, including those in the messy business of trying actually to make policies *happen* – and those who study and write about such matters. The tension and dialectic may be discerned from time to time in the chapters that follow. The active leadership of Pascal reflects as best it can this partnership; we endeavour to secure that the doers are in the driving seat.

The difficulty of holding this ring – after all scholars are paid to study and write about things to do with running the *civis* and its affairs rather than actually to carry them out – was offset for Pascal by the early recognition and frequent reaffirmation of a commonality of values and purposes behind often robust differences and confrontations on many matters. This commonality of purpose emerged gradually. It is made explicit in this introductory chapter, as well as being implicit in the tenor and assumptions of the chapters that follow.

The commonality centres on the simple proposition which lends itself to the title of this volume: that our global world and its competing nations and main institutions, both public and private sector, have become overly preoccupied with economics, and too unquestioningly bound to economic growth, to be able confidently to support the needs of a healthy, happy and sustainable set of societies. Behind the 'technology' of managing urban and regional planning, the build environment, and the many social services that vie for public and increasingly also for private resources, there lie more difficult questions about what matters most – and difficult technical questions about how one measures important but intangible factors like happiness.

Putting the economic in its place and practising partnership

How the *social* is understood is a political and ethical question, not one that can be asserted on the basis of technical argument alone. While recognising the legitimacy of different viewpoints, Pascal promotes a social agenda that sets out to address the causes and ameliorate the negative effects of social division and exclusion. It can advise policy-makers on cultural processes which are inclusive, in which people can make choices for themselves about quality of life and relationships, and about attaining and sustaining well-being. This is articulated preferably in collective, community terms, recognising the regional context.

Effective social policy formation requires recognition of the significance of learning. This learning is partly individual, but especially collective and organisational learning, as a means of understanding and addressing new policy challenges as they emerge. Learning involves sharing existing knowledge and openly experiencing knowledge-generation as a 'grounded' process. Knowledge-generation enables new strategies to be developed, and paradigms to shift, as unanticipated circumstances unfold or conflicts arise. Openness includes having the confidence and the ability to recognise policy failures and dead-ends, and to discuss and learn together from such experiences – something not all governments find easy, and that overly aggressive community groups do not necessarily facilitate.

Policy-makers need to understand that effective action on the *social* depends on respect for diversity, at least of culture and language, but for other differences also. Tolerance of diversity, like tolerance of ambiguity, does not come naturally to a tidy-minded bureaucracy. Interventions designed to 'rebalance' the *social* with the more narrowly economic cannot however be delivered by a single entity alone, whether a regional or local government, or even a large third-sector organisation.

Effective action relies on partnerships, which, to be effective, need to be able to:
- articulate a shared vision;
- mobilise resources, both money and people, commensurate with the objectives;
- establish coherent programmes, even in drawing on different agencies;
- build momentum, encouraging others to get involved;
- offer access to be included.

In order to deliver in this way, the following conditions need to be met in order for partnerships to be able to operate:
- the parties must recognise an agreed purpose and intended outcomes;
- each of the prospective partners needs to understand the others' standpoint(s);
- they must share a commitment to dialogue;
- there must be an open climate for the interchanges;
- there need to be transparent processes for decision-making.

Sound policy-making requires:
- a clear vision of desired outcomes;
- explicit understanding of the influence of values;
- access to reliable, grounded evidence;
- willingness to consult authentically with legitimate stake-holders;
- access to realistic resources;
- explicit frameworks for monitoring;
- agreed accountabilities.

These are the kinds of issues that Pascal exists to study, with close and sharp attention to understanding better in order to do better. Partnership across the sectors, like partnership (*joined-upness*) within government levels and portfolios vertically and horizontally, has become a *sine qua non* of success, as succeeding chapters in different ways suggest and explore. Pascal itself is a public and participatory experiment in partnership to which this volume also constitutes an invitation.

Threads through complexity

This volume draws on Pascal's first Hot Topics, cannibalised into a set of shorter chapters that together suggest issues and approaches served by the Observatory. They scratch the surface of the range of interconnected issues that must be addressed and comprehended in a joined-up way if we are to learn better self-governance for highly complex 'global' times.

Our intention in commissioning Hot Topics is to take up over time from different experiences, angles, country traditions and disciplinary (or more commonly trans-disciplinary) perspectives, various complex policy planning and implementing conundrums that are implied by the three points of the Pascal triangle – place management, social capital and the learning city region. Threading through all of these is the notion of lifelong learning that has been with us for something like 40 years. It has proved as frustrating and irritating in its ambiguous promiscuity as it has been fertile of new ways of thinking – more perhaps about life and society than about formal education.

This opening chapter reviews the range of themes thus addressed, implicitly also asking where the next phase of Pascal-mediated discourse and gathering of experience might usefully focus. The chapters that follow have mostly been developed from longer Hot Topics. These appeared originally on the Pascal website. Readers intrigued to trace origins, or who wish to consult elaborated versions of the stories, positions and propositions represented here, can visit that site for the longer versions (www.obs-pascal.com).

There is no inexorable logic to the sequence of their appearance, which differs from the order that follows here. We like and use the common metaphor of a jigsaw puzzle to illustrate the complex world in which we live. In chapter 2 Ron Faris plays with alternative notions of the Rubik's cube – a solvable puzzle – and the kaleidoscope, in attempting to characterise 'the emerging knowledge-based economy and society' in which 'the only constant is change'. The following chapters are pieces in a much bigger jigsaw than such a volume can contain: a puzzle with no fixed or straight edges, the shape of which will forever change, pieces of which will always be missing. Notwithstanding this, and reflecting an innate quest for logic and order, we begin with Faris' big-picture attempt to link the main elements in the Pascal mission before delving into social capital and the tensions it embodies and engenders. We then move on to questions about how to plan more participatively and with more self-renewing capacity: both in principle and as exemplified in different national-regional settings, concluding with the largest

challenge of all – the cultural change required to achieve sustainable development and with it ecological survival.

Implicit, but increasingly explicit as evidence accumulates and anxiety
mounts, is the notion of sustainability. This, like lifelong learning, has spilled
over the ecological and more narrowly environmental banks that initially
contained it, to flow into social and organisational life and management much
more broadly.

We do not pretend in this one volume to bring full understanding to such
complexity. Pascal's task is still more difficult: not just to try to understand or
to look for common values, reordered purposes and priorities, but to assist
decision-making and priority-setting of the kind that our book title suggests.
Pascal also attempts in tackling this to stimulate dialogue between scholars
and the policy-making community – between those who study things and
those who try to make them happen.

A distinctive feature and strength of this volume, therefore, is the way that its
contributors in many cases connect ideas with operations. Some are full-time
consultants, catalysts and change agents like Jim Cavaye and Ron Faris.
Others work in university settings, but with a keen instinct for and orientation
towards policy and the political; authors like Martin Mowbray and those
responsible for this introductory chapter. Others like Markku Sotaruata and
David Charles lead research programmes involved in learning city regions,
which require local engagement with the worlds of public and private
planning and enterprise. Shirley Walters has long been an architect-activist in
the making of the new South Africa, also straddling and sometimes erasing
the distinction between those who think and write and those who practise the
arts of politics and social change.

Alison StClair Baker and her colleagues in Kent work as planners – full-time
regional government bureaucrats if you wish – in a powerful Authority that
seeks to behave as a learning organisation by netting the best of new ideas and
putting them to work in running a virtual city region. Tom Healy, also now a
full-time bureaucrat at a national planning level, worked formerly in that highly
influential think-tank-cum-intergovernmental organisation (IGO), the OECD.
The OECD's innovative work, especially on learning regions, social capital and
lifelong learning, continues to influence and contribute to the work of Pascal.

In fact the OECD, a respectable and hard-nosed rich nations' economic club,
has been a source of many of the ideas that get an airing in this book. Without

offering an apologia for what is sometimes called the respectable face of the World Trade Organisation, International Monetary Fund and other unloved IGOs, this illustrates well the point behind our title in looking *beyond the economic* to the social and to sustainability. Lifelong learning looms large in OECD education sector thinking. That fact may confirm the conviction of some that lifelong learning has itself 'sold out to the capitalist way'. It may also however give pause for reflection. Alongside puzzle, paradox has its part to play in 'explaining the inexplicable' complexity of a complex changing world.

Ron Faris' chapter, which follows, offers a perspective from the West Coast of Canada on lifelong learning, tracing its lineage especially from Unesco and the OECD, and the way that it is connected with the 'sea of learning' on which education floats. He shows how the notion has been used federally and more locally in Canada, before considering in turn social capital, learning communities and regions, the less familiar notion of place management and the connections between them. This is tested out briefly here and in more detail in the longer Hot Topic paper, in the setting (or place) of Victoria, British Columbia. Challengingly, Faris concludes that we confront, for the indefinite future, not merely puzzle-solving but looking through a never-predicable kaleidoscope in which, unlike Rubik's Cube, there is no certain solution to be found, however long we persist.

The several succeeding chapters take us through a discussion of social capital, starting in Australia and moving to Europe. We begin with the attempt by Jim Cavaye to sketch out fairly coolly and objectively what social capital means, how it has been interpreted and how it has come to be deployed. He looks at its measurement, setting out issues to do with evaluation, benchmarks and indicators. Cavaye sought to stimulate a dialogue for Pascal, which opened through its website *forum* and provoked the response from fellow-Australian Martin Mowbray which takes the revised form of Chapter 4 and makes explicit the political dimensions that may often for comfort's sake be quietly ignored. Mowbray begins with the explicitly political in examining how Australia's federal 'dauphin', or heir apparent to the Prime Minister's throne, used 'social capital' as his 'big idea' ('nothing could be safer than a speech about social capital') before moving to a critical and clinical appraisal of the core Robert Putnam thesis and its aftermath. Mowbray concludes that, problematic as it is, the notion will not now go away. Instead he proposes 'social capital impact assessment' whereby the indirect – incidental, unintended and perverse – consequences of policies for social capital are explicitly and assiduously assessed.

John Field is one among several authors to have called attention elsewhere to the possible dark side of social capital; here he turns the spotlight onto the relationship between social networks and learning. His chapter reviews the nature of the relationship between innovation, learning and social capital, and he then considers some of the implications for policy and practice. In reviewing evidence from research, he points out that the relationship between these factors is not simple and is contingent on particular circumstances. The darkness refers to the intended and unintended outcomes of lifelong learning policies that create new learning divides and new or continuing social exclusion for those at greatest disadvantage. However, whilst acknowledging the darker side, he nevertheless suggests that the challenge is to determine what policies could be adopted if the ultimate goal is to make sustainability and justice central.

Concluding this group of papers, Tom Healy, writing in a personal capacity from the context of Irish national government in Dublin, but drawing on the very English tradition of the satirical *Yes Minister* and *Yes Prime Minister* TV series, offers a lively insight into the real and practical difficulties when the longer term and less tangible, less easily controlled, policy and governance attitudes and behaviours called for by social capital and social inclusion perspectives hit the brick wall of the urgent and no doubt often highly personalised, maybe career-driven, political imperatives of working politicians. More briefly than in the Hot Topic version (the text indicates by means of square brackets where a fuller discussion may be found), the chapter draws out some of the lessons contained in the conversation: about the limits of empirical research, the equality agenda and lifelong and experiential learning applied to social capital. He ends with Marx's dictum: that the point was not just to interpret the world but to change it.

In Chapter 7, by Markku Sotarauta, we stay with the difficulties inherent in the fact that real people with familiar complicated drives and motivations face huge complexity in managing in complex advanced industrial or knowledge societies. Naturally enough they tend to rely on their own and others' past experience of what works. The instinct to manage, direct and control, however, contradicts the need to mobilise wider resources and involve energies from all sectors; the need at local as well as national levels to co-manage complexities; and the need for continuous self-renewal at the heart of strategic adaptation.

Sotarauta's full Hot Topic takes as its title *Resilient City-Regions – Mission Impossible? Tales from Finland and Beyond about how to Build Self-*

Renewing Capacity. The anchorage in the stories of Tampere, Turku and other places gives traction to the more theoretical argument about the required attributes for self-renewal, although the author concedes in the Hot Topic that many more empirical studies are also required to test what he very convincingly proposes. The chapter ends on a sharp edge of challenge to policy-makers – stop chasing global buzzwords, look more to, and at, local issues and capabilities, serving rather than seeking to be served by these; and move from what he calls 'forcing' to 'real' partnership, scaling down the arrogance of 'policy wisdom' and entering into real and open dialogue.

We move from this rigorous analysis to two 'place-based' chapters, which tell how the county of Kent in England and the province of Western Cape in South Africa each attempt, in their own ways and their highly contrasting worlds, to behave like self-renewing learning regions that balance the inexorable demands for economic development with a rising imperative for social development, and indeed for sustainability in a richer quality of life. It is interesting to read these two thoroughly grounded real world accounts by reflective practitioners, both in their own right and through the lenses offered by Sotarauta. It will be very good if these quite self-revealing but not apologetic stories will encourage other policy-makers to reflect, using the channels and networks of Pascal, on how they go about their analogous duties, and how they recognise and learn from their own experience, as an end in itself and to be able to share it with others.

Universities feature significantly in the South African and (less prominently in what there is room for here) the Kent stories. Their engagement in the well-being of their societies, and especially of whatever is understood to be their natural regions or catchments, is the subject of Chapter 10. This addresses an important part of current policy debate about the role of universities and more broadly the relationship between formal education, social development and the learning society. What sometimes looks all too like a combat to the death between academic autonomy and relevance or utility has taken new forms as a quest for 'world-class', based on mainly scientific and technological research, is challenged by ideas about the 'engagement' of universities with their supporting communities as places for mutual sustenance in the generation and application of new knowledge.

David Charles leads the European Union funded CRITICAL project in which Sotarauta's Tampere is a partner. Working at the Centre for Urban and Regional Development Studies (CURDS) at the University of Newcastle in England's North-East, he is part of that country's most effective region (a sense of common economic history and difficulty, a shared culture, regional dialect and distinct identity) within England's quite recent attempt to achieve some devolution to a new nine-regions level. There is contest between a global reference point – world-class universities – and the reflected status that this gives the nation, and the effective involvement of (all) universities with their regions with a regional level of governance – through Lifelong Learning Networks to take just one recent initiative. Looking as an economic geographer from this regional perspective, Charles explores key aspects of this tension as higher education systems in all countries move rapidly from elite to the 'universal' status that knowledge societies appear to demand.

The volume concludes with a chapter prepared by Kate Sankey drawn from the very substantial Hot Topic contributed by Sara Parkin earlier this year on sustainable development. Hopefully many readers will be tempted from these 6,000 words to the full 35,000-word version where the issues and arguments sketched in this book are spelt out and referenced much more fully. Sustainability, like lifelong learning, is an often-abused term, devalued by careless use, applied to all kinds of politics, governance and organisational strategies as well as to the environmental crises that are at last penetrating the deafness of those who for comfort would not hear.

Like lifelong learning it is all but obligatory to acknowledge sustainability, but it is still usual to move on to seemingly more pressing and immediate – meaning both easier and more instantly politically convenient – matters. We make no apology for concluding with this clarion call. If communities and regions, from local to supra-national levels, cannot get this right – and like lifelong learning get it permeating all policy arenas – then the future will be bleak indeed.

Taking stock and moving on

The occasion for this volume is Pascal's third international conference, convened by the University of Stirling with NIACE, both founding Pascal partners. The genesis of the observatory was the OECD international conference in Melbourne, Australia three years earlier, that looked back at OECD's studies of European cities, drawn together in the volume called *Cities and Regions in the New Learning Economy* (OECD, 2001a). The Stirling conference opens with a review of what was found then, especially the ten policy principles, revisiting the five case studies of cities examined in the late 1990s. Together with the studies provided here, that Conference should assist us in taking stock of what more is now known, and what is thought and believed that is different, another five years on.

It has been a difficult opening to the new century. One conclusion implied by the task of bringing these papers together is that issues of value and principle, polarity, choice and possibly synthesis have become more acute. For us, the overweening domination of the economic over the social is among the most important of these tensions. If only in the interests of sustainability, rebalancing is necessary.

Chapter 2

Lifelong learning, social capital and place management: a Canadian perspective

Ron Faris

President, Golden Horizon Ventures, Victoria, British Columbia, Canada

Introduction

Three interrelated drivers of change are transforming our world. All three are the result of learning – the stem cell of a knowledge-based economy and society. The first driver, globalisation, is largely based on a market economy model and ideology characterised by short-term economic interest, privatisation of many social and economic functions previously carried out by the state, and deregulation of market rules. The transformation is enhanced by a second driver – the rapidly increasing pace of technological change sparked by research and innovation, especially in the information and communications technologies. The third driver is the explosion of new knowledge and learning – chiefly in the sciences and technologies – which has been harnessed to aid in the promotion of the first two drivers.

Whole nations, industries and communities have been changed by these forces that are rapidly impelling nations like Canada from resource-based to knowledge-based economies and societies. This chapter adopts a Canadian adult educator's perspective, drawing on both Canadian and global insights and experience.

In recent times Unesco and the OECD have promoted lifelong learning as a compass in the uncharted territory of the knowledge-based economy and society. One consequence has been an increased interest in learning community and region development by all levels of government in a number of jurisdictions.

After sketching key contributions to the development of the lifelong learning concept, this chapter considers several aspects of social and human capital theory and some links with lifelong learning. It emphasises the synergistic relationship between social and human capital, and the formal and non-formal learning dimensions of each – perspectives that have provided insight and impetus to the response of learning communities and regions to the powerful forces of globalisation.

It then illustrates how lifelong learning has served as the over-arching notion of an inter-disciplinary conceptual framework in a series of learning community and region projects in rural and urban British Columbia over the past five years. The framework is based on a perceived confluence of leading-edge political, economic, natural and social science, and community development theory and analysis that informs, and is informed by, both lifelong learning and social capital concepts. It provides an integrated, comprehensive, learning-based community response to the silos of government departments and the narrow disciplinary approaches of many academics.

In conclusion the chapter discusses the continuum of place management approaches and how lifelong learning and social capital concepts will contribute to place management practice in emerging initiatives in Victoria, British Columbia. Together, these concepts provide important insights into our complex, diverse, and changing communities and regions, but raise the question whether the many moving parts of learning communities could best be viewed as a solvable Rubik's Cube or an ever-changing kaleidoscope.

Lifelong learning

Why has the notion of lifelong learning so often been used in a confused and confusing way? A brief survey of the development of the concept, and of related lifelong education and adult education may assist in answering these questions.

Some historic roots

Earlier thought influenced the definition, principles and use of the terms lifelong education and lifelong learning. The Anglo-Saxon use of these terms is rooted in the adult education movement. As early as 1919 the Report of the Adult Education Committee of the UK Ministry of Reconstruction asserted that:

(A)dult education must not be regarded as a luxury for a few exceptional persons here and there, not as a thing which concerns a short span of early manhood, but that adult education is a permanent national necessity, an inseparable aspect of citizenship, and therefore should be both universal and lifelong.

In 1926 Eduard Lindeman (1961) argued that 'education is life, not merely preparation for an unknown kind of future living, the whole of life is learning, therefore education can have no endings'. In 1929 Basil Yeaxlee authored *Lifelong Education*, the first book explicitly devoted to the concept. Thus, in the English-speaking world the notions of lifelong education and adult education became inextricably bound – nowhere more clearly than in Canada where notable adult educators, among them Roby Kidd and Alan Thomas, promoted both concepts and were among those who gradually transformed the notion of lifelong education into lifelong learning. Kidd was President of the Second Unesco International Conference on Adult Education in Montreal in 1960 that set lifelong education as a goal for the future policies of governments (Himmelstrup, 1981). In 1961 Alan Thomas (1963b) addressed the Ottawa conference of the Canadian Association for Adult Education on the Learning Society, arguing that the capacity for learning should be the foundation of Canadian society:

We therefore offer as our central concern, not education, in its formal and institutional sense, but learning. Whatever the explicit and various goals of the multitude of agencies which we here are associated with or represent, we have one common concern, the ability of human beings to learn continuously, and the conditions under which learning best takes place. These conditions are the foundations of the learning society.

Kidd (1978, 1980), who had edited a dozen booklets in the 1950s with the series title *Lifelong Learning* discussed principles to govern the organisation of lifelong learning. In his 1966 Quance lecture, 'Organizing for Lifelong Learning', Kidd (1978) noted that 'lifelong learning' was not a synonym for adult education, but the distinction was not universally accepted. Himmelstrup (1981) pointed out:

Until the late 1970s many people (including decision makers) thought that Lifelong Education was almost a synonym with 'adult education'… And as adult education notoriously finds itself in a weak and marginal position in most countries, it has been very difficult to give the necessary force to make a political breakthrough.

The international scene: some key episodes

Philosophical and ideological differences influenced the use of the terms lifelong education and lifelong learning in different regions and nations as early as the mid-1960s. Two concepts, *education permanente* and *recurrent education*, provided alternative notions. In the 1960s Paul Lengrand initiated discussion of *education permanente* that influenced thinking in the Council of Europe, especially when its Council for Cultural Cooperation investigated the notion during the 1970s (Hilmmelstrup,1981; Kidd, 1980). Northern European political leaders, led by the Olaf Palme, then Sweden's Minister of Education, promoted recurrent education. The OECD fostered discussion of this concept of alternation between the worlds of education and work throughout an individual's lifetime.

American attempts in the mid-1970s to build a federal lifelong learning and education initiative, the Mondale *Lifelong Learning Act*, were stillborn with the election of the Reagan administration, which in 1984 withdrew from Unesco for alleged financial mis-management and an 'anti-American agenda'. The following year the UK Thatcher government also withdrew. Britain was to return in 1997, the US in 2002. During the intervening period a generation of American and British educators, unlike Canadians, did not formally participate in Unesco's concept development and application related to lifelong learning and education. This breakdown in networking, trust and shared values – social capital – among English-speaking adult educators was problematic and may have led to greater definitional and semantic diversity in a field characterised by competition over concepts and terminology.

Unesco

Unesco's international leadership in the discussion of lifelong education and learning was assured with the publication of Lengrand's *An Introduction to Lifelong Education* (1970) and the report of its International Commission on the Development of Education (Faure report), *Learning to Be* (Unesco, 1972). A main theme of the Faure report was the need to develop a wider concept of education, both lifelong and life-wide, and of a learning society in which the non-formal sector and the individual self-directed learner would play an increasing role: it was more productive to view individual and national development from the perspective of learning than from that of formal education.

R. H. Dave, as Director of the Unesco Institute for Education in Hamburg, led theoretical development of the concept of lifelong education particularly related to adult basic education. He defined lifelong education as:

> a comprehensive concept which includes formal, non-formal and informal learning extended throughout the lifespan of an individual to attain the fullest possible development in personal, social and professional life. It seeks to view education in its totality and includes learning that occurs in the home, school, community, and workplace, and through the mass media and other situations and structures for acquiring and enhancing enlightenment. (Himmelstrup, 1981, p.19)

During 1996, the European Year of Lifelong Learning of the European Union, Unesco issued the report of a three-year global consultation chaired by Jacques Delors. *Learning: the Treasure Within* (Unesco, 1996) claimed that 'learning throughout life will be one of the keys to meeting the challenges of the twenty-first century'.

Several key concepts related to the Unesco notion of lifelong learning are:
- a life-span (birth to death) or vertical dimension;
- a life-wide or horizontal dimension manifested in the different settings of learning through a lifetime (home, community, school and work place) and across societal sectors (governance, economic, public, education and community/voluntary);
- a distinction between the formal learning sector (credentialised education and training) and the equally important non-formal learning sector (purposeful non-credentialised learning in the home, community and workplace); and
- a comprehensive range of social, cultural and economic purposes for individual and organisational learning.

OECD

In 1973 the OECD report on *Recurrent Education: A Strategy for Lifelong Learning* defined recurrent education as a:

> comprehensive educational strategy for all post-secondary or post-basic education, the essential characteristic of which is the distribution of education over the total life span of the individual in a recurring way, i.e. the alternation with other activities such as work, but also leisure and retirement.

This and subsequent documents promoted mechanisms such as paid educational leave that were implemented in a number of western Europe nations and inspired serious investigation in Canada, but gained little acceptance in the UK and the USA (Kidd, 1980; Department of Education and Science, 1973).

The European Year of Lifelong Learning saw the publication of OECD's *Lifelong Learning for All* (1996). The report, for the OECD Education Committee at Ministerial level, concluded that the 'Ministers accepted lifelong learning for all as the guiding principle for policy strategies ... to improve the capacity of individuals, families, workplaces and communities to adapt and renew'. It is based on a view of learning that:

> embraces individual and social development of all kinds and in all settings – formally, in schools, at home, at work, and in the community. The approach is system-wide; it focuses on the standards of knowledge and skills needed by all, regardless of age. It emphasizes the need to prepare and motivate all children at an early age for learning over a lifetime, and directs efforts to ensure that all adults, employed and unemployed, who need to retrain or upgrade their skills are provided the opportunity to do so. As such it is geared to serve several objectives:
> * to foster personal development, including the use of time outside of work (including retirement);
> * to strengthen democratic values;
> * to cultivate community life;
> * to maintain social cohesion; and
> * to promote innovation, productivity and economic growth.

OECD's 2001 *Cities and Regions in the New Learning Economy* analyses the role of individual and organisational learning in learning regions, including five case studies of regions responding to the challenge of the emerging knowledge-based or learning economy. There is a focus on 'the relationships between the development of regional systems on innovation and the processes of individual learning. The latter are embodied in learning processes that embrace formal educational organizations and sites of informal learning in families and communities; as well as firms and other workplaces, universities and R & D organizations' (OECD, 2001a).

Other regional activities
OECD and Unesco initiatives have been informed and animated by several

major regional bodies. In 1997 the Asia-Pacific Economic Cooperation (Hatton, 1997) commissioned a Canadian-led survey of the lifelong learning concept and its application. The 1999 G8 Cologne Summit developed a charter – *Aims and Ambitions for Lifelong Learning* – which noted that 'economies and societies are increasingly knowledge-based. Educational skills are indispensable to achieving economic success, civic responsibility and social cohesion, requiring:

- a renewed commitment to investment in lifelong learning;
- identifying the essential elements of a lifelong learning strategy; and
- using international good practice as the building blocks for educational reform.

The 2000 G8 Education Minister's Meeting in Tokyo asserted that:

> Education policy cannot be developed nor practice shaped in isolation. There must be consistency and connections between primary, secondary and tertiary education, resulting in true lifelong learning systems. There must also be consistency and connections with other policy domains such as employment, science, technology and information and communication. There must be engagement in implementation with society as a whole and with local communities.

While, like Unesco and the OECD, the G8 focused on education system reform, the links between social and economic policy and the increasingly important role of information technologies in the emerging knowledge-based society were also highlighted.

A year-long Commission of European Communities consultation in 2000–2001 followed the 2000 *Memorandum on Lifelong Learning* (2000). The six key areas included 'provision of lifelong learning opportunities as close to learners as possible, in their own communities and supported through information technologies wherever appropriate'.

The Commission, which has subsequently encouraged support for learning communities, cities and regions, has thus, like the G8, adopted a comprehensive, coherent definition of lifelong learning that recognises the importance of local communities as the settings of learning (European Commission, 2001).

Some Canadian perspectives

Several provinces contributed to growing interest in and application of lifelong learning principles at community or regional levels. A Saskatchewan Association for Lifelong Learning (SALL) was formed in 1971 and pressed for a unique community college model based on lifelong and community education principles. A Minister's Advisory Committee on Community Colleges, with a majority of SALL members, was charged with a community consultation process resulting in a unique 'made-in-Saskatchewan' college model. The two key assumptions of the report were:

> The sense of community in rural Saskatchewan, built on traditions of community participation and co-operation blended with self help, is among the province's most valuable attributes, and

> Learning continues throughout life and access to learning opportunities should be continuous.

> … They [key assumptions] underlie all other assumptions — that learning is a vital and necessary part of life as both a personal and social experience and that communities as well as individuals require new information and attitudes to meet new and changing conditions. (Saskatchewan, 1972)

This combination of social capital and lifelong learning resulted in a novel college brokerage model that was to engage in community development and education as well as deliver a full range of academic and vocational pro-grammes. An associated study, *The Saskmedia Report* (Saskatchewan, 1973), recommended the integrated development of an educational communications system with the existing provincial public library and emerging community college systems.

College development and reform in British Columbia was also influenced by lifelong learning concepts. The report of the Task Force on the Community College (British Columbia, 1974), entitled *Towards the Learning Community*, claimed that:

> Learning is a natural and necessary human activity that should not and cannot be confined to educational institutions. It is a life-long process which occurs in real-life situations of the community as well as in educational facilities. A fundamental

purpose of a community college therefore, is to provide learning opportunities and encourage learning throughout the wider community as well as within college walls.

The Task Force foresaw new community links being forged as the colleges, among other roles:

- engage in community educational developmental services actively participating in the communities by assisting individuals and organizations 'in promoting a greater sense of community and in developing community resources';
- act as information clearing-houses for adult education programmes conducted by community organizations; and
- provide access to media-communications services for community groups and individuals.

These proposed community capacity and social capital building roles were largely untested as the new conservative government abandoned plans for implementing all the recommendations related to community development. A generation later, with election of a more progressive provincial government, lifelong learning once again was on the public agenda. A 1992 report, *Lifelong Learning for the 21st Century*, called for development of a lifelong learning policy and administrative framework including:

- adopting 'the concept of lifelong learning as an organizing principle and social goal for education and training programs of all government ministries and agencies, the total public education system, and the promotion of learning opportunities in the non-formal sector, and that such a view be incorporated in a provincial policy statement'; and
- creation of independent community learning councils composed of formal and non-formal sector stakeholders that would initiate and fund programmes such as multi-cultural and citizenship education; local economic development; solutions of social problems; family learning; health and safety education, and volunteer training (British Columbia, 1992).

Inter-Ministry rivalries, and serial changes in the incumbent of the Premier's Office were among political and bureaucratic reasons for inaction on the report's major recommendations.

Canadian federal government initiatives

Despite sporadic attempts of authorities in some provinces to apply the concept of lifelong learning to the reform of their education and training systems in the 1970s onward, no major initiatives of the Canadian federal government commenced until the 1991 consultation paper *Learning Well ... Living Well*, part of an attempted joint constitutional and socio-economic reform by the Progressive Conservative government of the day. The paper proposed building structures for a system of lifelong learning that would network the many components of a learning system that it claimed largely already existed, albeit in an incoherent manner (Canada, 1991). Defeat of the constitutional reform package in a national referendum a year later spelled doom for the associated lifelong learning initiative.

Almost a decade later a Liberal federal government commenced initiatives, chiefly through its Human Resources Development Canada (HRDC) department, that were informed by aspects of the lifelong learning concept. The 1999 Speech from the Throne promised 'a national action plan on skills and learning for the 21st Century that will focus on lifelong learning, address the challenge of poor literacy among adults, and provide citizens with the information they need to make good decisions about developing their skills' (Canada, 1999). That year the HRDC's Office of Learning Technologies commenced funding of Community Learning Networks initiative that would forward the Office's mandate to 'promote a lifelong learning culture in Canada'.

In 2001 Teresa MacNeil, a noted adult educator, conducted the most comprehensive analysis of the state of lifelong learning policy ever undertaken in Canada (MacNeil, 2001). She found a largely uncoordinated and incoherent approach to formal education and training across the nation. She concluded that the term lifelong learning was not well understood and was often equated with formal adult education to the exclusion of non-formal learning. Comprehensive lifelong learning objectives, the essence of a learning culture, had yet even to be suggested through public policy in Canada. In the absence of coordinating mechanisms in any jurisdiction 'coordination may only be possible at the community level where all services can be brought together and where the individual learner can be the focus of attention'.

A national think-tank on learning communities convened by the Learning Policy Directorate of HRDC in 2003 illustrated a new interest not only in a more comprehensive definition of lifelong learning but also in learning communities and regions. The role of lifelong learning and social capital concepts in development of learning communities and regions were central seminar themes.

Education floats upon a sea of learning

The concept of lifelong learning is based upon the recognition that learning – the acquisition of knowledge, skills, attitudes and values – is a natural everyday process that occurs throughout one's life. It is driven by human curiosity and intelligence that attempts to give meaning to information in all its forms. It is both an individual activity and a social process that occurs in all of life's stages from birth to death. Most of the learning we acquire is from or with others.

There is also a life-wide dimension that recognises that systematic learning occurs not only in the formal sector for credentials but also the non-formal sector or context of the workplace and the voluntary or community setting (Colley et al., 2002). Finally, informal or non-systematic, but often purposeful, learning can occur as one views television, or discusses politics around the family table or gardening tips with a neighbour.

Lifelong learning is a seamless process by which we all can learn better to perform roles as active citizens and community participants, effective parents and family members, productive workers and informed consumers, and creative learners. It may be a mixed blessing if, while it raises aspirations and invokes novel policy debate, it serves to further exclude and alienate (Field, 2000). Another view is that 'there is a rich and strong meaning to the notion of lifelong learning which is worth promoting and expressing in policy and institutional behaviour' (Duke, 2002).

Several experts have identified different stages or 'generations' of conceptual development. Rubenson (2001) argues that the first of three generations occurred from the late 1960s to the early 1970s and viewed 'lifelong learning as a master concept and guiding principle for restructuring education' with a major role for the civil society. Interest reappeared in the late 1980s with an emphasis on 'economic restructuring and international competitiveness through increased productivity' focused on the role of the market. The third and present generation, commenced in 2000, sees a balance among the 'different roles for and interrelations between the three major institutional arrangements, state, market and civil society' and stresses the aims of active citizenship and employability. Duke (2002) identifies two phases. The first, starting in the 1960s and lasting just over a decade, 'remained a relatively erudite conversation limited to policy and academic circles'. The second began in the early nineties and not only popularised the term but also saw it become 'increasingly a tool for the reform and modernisation of aspects of national education and training systems' (Field, 2001; Duke, 2002).

Lifelong education is limited to the contribution of the formal sector in providing credit-based education and training opportunities for individuals throughout their lifespan. It means that individuals will play student roles – characterised by dependency and competitive individualism – as they enrol in formal institutions. In contrast, those who engage in non-formal learning play member roles characterised by learning-in-community or social learning that strengthen the organisations, communities and families in which the learning occurs (Thomas, 1963a).

Lifelong and adult education are lifelong learning's fraternal but non-identical twins. They have to this day been seen in some jurisdictions and by some discussants as synonymous with lifelong learning. In reality lifelong and adult education are encompassed by the concept of lifelong learning. Adult education overlaps the concept of lifelong education. Lifelong education recognises the formal educational opportunities that children, youth and adults engage in, while adult education focuses on the formal, non-formal and informal learning opportunities of adults, however adulthood may be culturally defined. Learning is the common denominator of both lifelong and adult education. Education 'floats upon a sea of learning' (Thomas, 1987).

Social capital

Introduction
The link between the concept of social capital and education is historic. According to Robert Putnam the term 'social capital' was first coined by an American state supervisor of rural schools, L.J. Hanifan, in 1916 to emphasise the importance of community involvement for successful schools (Putnam, 2000).

The concept of human capital was a subject of substantial debate in the 1960s when it first entered the global stage. Today it is firmly established and recognised by mainstream economists. Social capital has caught on over the past decade. Robert Putnam's classic, *Bowling Alone: The Collapse and Revival of American Community* (2000), placed the concept at the centre of the policy agenda. It remains contested and increasing attention is being given to both its definition and measurement (Cavaye, 2004).

Link to human capital and lifelong learning
The OECD has recognised the value of combining human and social capital analysis within the context of lifelong learning. Several OECD reports have

investigated aspects of this synergistic relationship: one looked at the effects in the six learning regions projects conducted from 1997 to 2000 (OECD, 2001a); another, *The Well-being of Nations: The Role of Human and Social Capital*, 'identified the roles of human and social capital in realizing sustainable economic and social development' (OECD, 2001b). The report recognised both life-span and life-wide dimensions of human capital development:

> Learning and acquisition of skills and knowledge takes place from birth to death. The concept of lifelong learning emphasizes not just the importance of adult learning and training, but also learning at all stages of life including 'learning to learn' in the context of schools and other institutions of formal education: both the lifelong and 'life-wide'. Human capital is developed in the contexts of:
> - learning, within the family and early childcare settings;
> - formal education and training including early childhood, school-based compulsory education, post-compulsory vocational or general education, tertiary education, public labour market training, adult education, etc.;
> - workplace training as well as informed [sic informal] learning at work through specific activities such as research and innovation or participation in various professional networks;
> - informal learning 'on-the-job' and in daily living and civic participation.

This seminal report defines human capital as 'the knowledge, skills, competencies and attribute embodied in individuals that facilitate the creation of personal, social and economic well-being', and defines social capital as 'networks together with shared norms, values and understandings that facilitate co-operation within or among groups'. It distinguishes social from both human and physical capital as being relational rather than the exclusive property on an individual; a public good shared by a group; produced by societal investments of time and effort albeit in a less direct manner than human or physical capital; and a product of inherited culture and norms of behaviour.

The report concludes that human and social capital are mutually reinforcing; both are 'created, formally and informally, in the workplace, in local communities, and within families' rightly noted as important learning environments.

According to Putnam (2000) social capital has powerful effects upon:

- child development;
- student academic performance from school to college levels; and
- community involvement in schools.

Balatti and Falk (2001) argue that:

> Social capital building is implicated in effective adult learning in three most important ways:
> 1. Social capital is involved in program design, management and delivery whether it is explicitly recognized as such or not. Its explicit recognition facilitates superior planning and delivery.
> 2. The processes of drawing on and building social capital are part and parcel of the learning process.
> 3. Social capital can be a direct or indirect benefit of learning.

A recent UK survey of social capital concludes that:

> Social capital may prove to be the single most important variable to impact educational attainment, with much greater importance than the resources conventionally focused on, but further work needs to be conducted to establish causal direction at macro-level. (UKPIU, 2002)

One aspect of synergistic social and human capital development that has resonance in communities, particularly where local and traditional knowledge is valued, is the social-historical dimension of learning. Learning is a cumulative social and cultural process for our species. Historical analysis can give insight into both its social and human capital development consequences (Szreter, 2000; Thurow, 2000; UKPIU, 2002). This is particularly true in aboriginal communities, which hold a significantly different world view to people in the dominant society. They identify themselves as the first people of a region (known in Canada as the First Nation) with a profound affinity to the land and an accumulation of insights, wisdom and knowledge and skills passed on by successive generations of elders. Lifelong learning, and especially informal, experiential learning is central to how they have learned and continue to learn (Wotherspoon and Butler, 1999; Burns, 1998; Haig-Brown, 2000). Recognition of this knowledge and value system is especially important in places where aboriginal people continue to live and learn.

Schuller, acknowledging the contribution of human capital theory to the idea of education as an investment, claims that 'it has to be complemented by an approach [social capital] which underlines the recognition that learning is a social activity and depends for its value on its embeddedness within a social framework' (Schuller, 1998). He underscores the importance of people learning together in informal associations as well as in formal settings. A recent study of the contribution of adult formal and non-formal learning to social capital concludes that 'there is strong evidence that adult learning contributes to changes in attitudes and behaviours that promote social capital and, possibly, social cohesion' (Feinstein et al., 2003).

Non-formal learning is fostered in the wide array of voluntary associations that exist in our communities. Learning acquired through volunteer work is a major motivation for many volunteers who wish to gain new skills (Ross and Shillington, 1990; Canada, 1998). Studies in Canada and Australia indicate that over 70 per cent of the learning in workplaces is of a non-formal or informal nature (Falk and Kilpatrick, 1999; Livingston, 2000; Sousa and Quarter, 2003). Thus it is in communities – the families, workplaces, voluntary associations and educational institutions therein – that most of the learning associated with building trust, networks and shared values occurs.

Learning communities and regions

There has been steady growth of learning community initiatives around the world since the 1992 OECD conference launched the concept in Gothenberg, Sweden. Development of several learning cities in the UK in the mid-1990s and the subsequent creation of a UK *Learning Cities Network* (recently re-named the *Learning Communities Network*) influenced development in a growing number of initiatives in the Anglo-Saxon world, including Australia, New Zealand and Canada.

OECD and UK experience strongly influenced the evolution of a structural/process learning community model in British Columbia.

Learning communities in British Columbia
In 1999 the first of a number of learning communities was created in rural British Columbia. The federal Office of Learning Technologies of Human Resources Development Canada (HRDC) cooperated with the then provincial Ministry of Community Development, Cooperatives and Volunteers to

promote learning community development. Both provided funding for developmental work with potential project communities and developed an initial working agreement as a framework for future initiatives.

In the first years the concepts of lifelong learning and social capital in a variety of communities were applied and work began on a learning-based approach to community development (Faris and Peterson, 2000; Faris, 2001), with a framework in which lifelong learning is the organising principle and social goal. It draws upon a growing body of inter-disciplinary research and analysis from the natural and social sciences including:

- ecological models from the biological and environmental sciences that provide insights into holistic, sustainable life systems (Capra, 1996, 2002; Natrass and Altomare, 1999);
- human development research especially from the population health and neurosciences that emphasise the importance of investing in early learning strategies that have lifelong impacts (Mustard and Keating,1993; Keating and Hertzman, 1999);
- an emerging political economy that recognises the contribution and synergy of human and social capital in a knowledge-based economy (Szreter, 1999, 2000); and
- associated communitarian values that stress the need for active citizens, communities empowered by education and new technologies, and the use of social capital to foster local economic development and social cohesion (Etzioni, 1994).

Learning communities explicitly use lifelong learning concepts to enable local people from every community sector to act together to enhance the social, economic, cultural and environmental conditions of their community. It is a pragmatic, asset-based approach that mobilises the learning resources and expertise of all five community sectors:

- civic or local government;
- economic (private and social enterprise);
- public (libraries, recreation commissions, social agencies, arts councils, health bodies, museums etc.);
- education (nursery to university); and
- voluntary/community.

The total formal (nursery, school, college and university) and non-formal (civic, economic, public and voluntary) learning resources of a community are therefore harnessed for immediate impacts as well as longer-term consequences according to the needs and priorities set by the community. In every community prior or current local initiatives are recognised and built upon by the nascent learning community.

The determinants of success, initially drawn from a UK study (DfEE, 1999), were borne out in this experience. That is, the success of each project depends upon the degree to which each community can learn to:

- build partnerships and networks within and among all five community sectors;
- foster participation of all citizens, including the most disadvantaged; and
- assess project performance and progress in achieving community-set targets.

The concept of lifelong learning has served a multitude of uses in enabling learning communities to make a difference.

Seven uses of the lifelong learning concept in British Columbia's learning communities

The lens of lifelong learning has been used in various ways at the developmental and implementation stages of British Columbia's learning communities. It guides the creation of community socio-economic profiles that provide a shared, agreed-upon database for community discussion and a benchmark for project progress. It provides the framework for mapping and assessing a community's assets including its social and human capital – intangible assets of a sustainable learning community in an emerging knowledge-based society. It enables the lifespan needs of individuals and groups and the life-wide settings of family, workplace and community to be assessed. It fosters recognition of the life-wide learning resources of all five community sectors in their respective 'silos' to be mobilised for the common good.

Lifelong learning is thus a vision of a possible future to which a community aspires, enabling a cluster of inter-related functions and purposes, including:

- a. a means of identifying needs and prioritising action;
- b. an analytical/planning tool for community asset mapping;
- c. a comprehensive approach to transformative learning;
- d. a means of promoting social inclusion;
- e. an important link with social/human capital generation;
- f. an incubator for citizenship and leadership development; and
- g. a means of sustainable economic, environmental and social change.

Place management

Introduction

Place management is a relatively new concept of community service delivery
with its origins chiefly in the field of urban planning and government practice
in the UK and such Australian states as New South Wales and Queensland
(Stewart-Weeks, 1998, 2000; Zappala and Green, 2001). The term *place*
denotes a geographically-bounded location whether a human settlement such
as a neighbourhood, town, city, region or a larger political unit such as a state
or inter-state entity, or a geographically defined landscape such as a river
basin or ecological region. The term *management* is contested.

Management as a command and control function is universally rejected in
place management thinking. Providing whole-of-government responses to
social, economic and environmental issues in specific localities is the
generally accepted core management objective. Coordinated or integrated
delivery of public services to geographic communities or place is a major
goal. An array of projects across the globe illuminate contributions of the
concept and its links to both lifelong learning and social capital theory.

Australia

Place management projects have occurred over a decade in Australia, led by
the New South Wales Strengthening Local Communities Unit housed in the
Premier's Department, which promotes place management policy and
practice throughout the State. The Unit provides policy and project development, training and consultancy service including an electronic Place Management Network. In 2001 a consultation with stakeholders focused on a training
strategy and also attempted to develop a consensus about key features of the
approach with the following definition:

> A place management or community renewal programme is one
> which generally exhibits the following features:
> - it is project based;
> - projects focus on specific communities (neighbourhoods,
>   towns, or remote areas);
> - projects aim to address key social or economic issues which
>   seriously impact on general community well-being;
> - projects promote a cross Government agency approach to
>   planning and services provision, and, in some cases, an active
>   cross sector approach;
> - project practices, if proven effective, should be informing

long term, significant changes to the core planning and service provision activities of agencies, and partnerships with other sectors, within communities.

Observers of place management projects in New South Wales and Queensland find a continuum of place management possibilities. Stuart-Weeks (1998) distinguishes between place coordination (improved service delivery), place management (significant changes about decision-making, projects funding and accountability) and place leadership (response to demand for increased community governance).

A Smith Family working paper (Zappala and Green, 2001) sees *place coordination* (minimal change to existing government service delivery) at one end of a spectrum and *place entrepreneurship* (community-based approaches involving government, business and non-profit organisations) at the other. The paper critiques several place management projects of the New South Wales Government, concluding that *place coordination* is best left to government but that *place entrepreneurship* approaches are best led by non-profit and community organisations, especially since such groups are immune from short-term political cycles. This would be ideal but is unrealistic in Canada where short-term project or 'drive-by funding' equally plagues government and non-governmental organisations and the communities they would serve.

Place management project – Victoria, British Columbia

The City of Victoria, capital of British Columbia, has a population of about 80,000 people but a dozen surrounding municipalities account for a further 200,000 plus. A *Vision 2020* initiative, sparked by the Downtown Business Association, commenced in November 2003. The initiative formed a *Place of Learning* sub-committee composed of leaders from the civic, economic, education and public library sectors, including the author, which developed tentative objectives for a 2020 Vision of Victoria as a leading learning community.

In April 2004 the City of Victoria Corporate Strategic Plan incorporated an objective to *Promote Downtown as a Place of Learning*. One recommendation is for the city to adopt a place management, that is, whole of civic government, social entrepreneurship strategy. This project may entail focusing whole of civic level government resources (for example, education, police, social services, libraries and community development, including social housing) on a collaborative basis involving downtown stakeholders in order to achieve agreed-upon *Vision 2020* goals. The city council's proclamation of Victoria as a Learning City in April 2005 was followed in May by the creation of the Mayor's Task Force on a Learning Commons.

Summary

There are social, historical, ecological, cultural and political economic dimensions to the evolving concept of place management. The politically and culturally acceptable operational definition of management may well vary by jurisdiction. The definition most consistent with learning region values is for a management style that facilitates networking and partnership building, increases the stock of human and social capital, and enables learning for sustainable social, environmental and economic development. Those who govern in jurisdictions where aboriginal people reside have a special challenge to listen and learn from, and work with a people with a rich sense of place.

While *place entrepreneurship* models will enable cross-sectoral collaboration, which increases the probability of long-term sustainability, the issue of short-term 'drive-by' funding is central. How can issues that have grown over several generations be addressed in one or even three year funded projects? For example, family breakdown among aboriginal people who, for several generations, were raised in residential schools in Canada or Australia rather than in their own families has had profound inter-generational consequences. It may take at least a generation to heal the wounds and learn the skills and attitudes necessary to rebuild the families and communities of those victimised by an insensitive dominant society.

Rubik's Cube or kaleidoscope?

In the emerging knowledge-based economy and society the only constant is change. Those who try to bridge the theory and practice of learning-based community development in learning communities and regions recognise how complex, diverse, and changing communities are.

It is an incredibly complex and daunting challenge to assess the multiple dimensions of human communities and their connection to other living systems. In the search for stories, parables and metaphors to help us understand, we may ask whether the many moving parts of learning regions are akin to a giant Rubik's Cube or more like a giant kaleidoscope.

Rubik's Cube is a solvable puzzle. By adeptly changing one component after another, what initially appears a nest of confusion becomes an ordered pattern. Each time a component is moved the total relationship changes. Each move is made with subsequent moves in mind. With experiential learning and abstract thought the puzzle is solved. Can we transfer the ability to predict the consequences of changes, even several iterations of compounded change, to a community? The need for constant re-evaluation and re-alignment is applicable to place management. Can we predict the cascading consequences of wilful moves after each re-evaluation so that the solution can be approached despite the moves introduced by other uncontrollable forces within a community?

A kaleidoscope is a tubular viewing device containing two plane mirrors and multiple coloured fragments. When the instrument is rotated it forms ever-changing patterns. Its attraction is the colourful diversity and unpredictable nature of the patterns produced. Place management projects – particularly of a *place entrepreneurship* nature – that use lifelong learning and social capital concepts to foster resilient learning communities may be more akin to using a kaleidoscope than a Rubik's Cube: requisite problem-solving entails no final solution, but rather the constant challenge of learning our way out by infusing policies and practice with learning strategies for all those involved – from place managers and bureaucrats to community members. Formulaic responses to dynamic and unique community conditions cannot replace learning-based capacity building.

All metaphors have their limitations including these two. Yet both illuminate challenges we face as associated elements of the three concepts of lifelong learning, social capital, and place management – the power of non-formal learning and its parity with formal learning, and the importance of joining up the horizontal learning resources of government with those of the life-wide sectors of the community – inform efforts to achieve whole-of-government and whole-of-community approaches to tackling economic, social and environmental issues in learning regions.

In the best Canadian tradition of compromise, should I opt for a Rubik's Kaleidoscope, or simply foster discussion about the possible contribution of both these or other metaphors? In a knowledge-based economy and society, and in the places where we live and learn, the future seems more like a kaleidoscope of ever-changing challenges than a Rubik's Cube where there is a certain solution. Chaos and complexity may be our lot. In this human condition our capacity to learn-in-community, and to celebrate differences and creativity, will be crucial to the task of enabling whole people to live in whole communities of the future.

Chapter 3

Social capital: a commentary on issues, understanding and measurement

Jim Cavaye

Director, Cavaye Community Development, Toowoomba, Australia

Many community workers and citizens have understood, perhaps intuitively, the importance of networks, trust and cooperation in communities for decades. Yet, social capital retains many interpretations and expectations. It remains hard for policy analysts to grasp: government and the private sector often struggle to see it as part of core business; measuring social capital requires sophistication and flexibility; and a service delivery culture in many agencies and businesses struggles to incorporate it.

This paper raises issues and questions about social capital and focuses on approaches to measuring and assessing social capital in communities.

What we know about social capital

The nature of social capital has many interpretations with considerable debate about its characteristics and function. Some common characteristics of social capital in the literature are:
- participation in networks;
- reciprocity;
- trust;
- social Norms;
- a sense of the 'commons';
- proactivity and cooperation.

Coleman (1988) described social capital as 'inhering in the structure of relations between actors and among actors'. Flora and Flora (1993) saw social capital as entrepreneurial social infrastructure consisting of diversity, resource mobilisation and the quality of networks in communities. Granovetter (1973) and Lin (1988) stressed the importance of 'weak ties' between people as social networks develop in communities.

Other general understandings of social capital are as follows:

- Social capital consists of three related forms – bonding, bridging and linking (Woolcock, 1999).
- Social capital interacts with other forms of capital. For example, Schmid and Robison (1995) found that social capital affected prices, the acceptance of risk, the choice of leasing contracts, loan approval and bank loyalty.
- Communities have large reserves of latent social capital. During crises such as bushfire or flood, community members readily participate and interact.
- Social capital is both a means and an end. As a means, it mediates relationships and participation. As an end, the relationships and networks that mediate action become strengthened in themselves.
- Social capital increases as community people 'use' it, and it decreases if they don't use it.
- Putnam (1993b) suggested that social capital tends to be polarised with communities moving towards opposite ends of a spectrum of social capital.
- Social capital fundamentally involves values. Social capital supports the values that community members want to uphold in their community.

The 'dark side'

Social networks are embedded in different sectors of communities and social capital can support unhealthy norms. It can reinforce existing cleavages in communities and lead to social cartels prone to corruption (Putnam, 1995). Social networks can also lock people into declining social sectors such as ethnic groups involved in low wage informal work (Edwards and Foley, 1997). In communities with a culture of illicit drug use, social norms can ostracise community members acting to change their circumstances (Portes, 1998).

Social capital can also sanction the civic action of community members and fortify unjust community power structures. For example, Putnam (1995) suggests that the declining racial discrimination in middle-class America since the 1950s may well be related to the erosion of social capital that upheld discriminatory norms.

Issues and questions

Levels of social capital
I contend that social capital could be considered at four levels:
1. Individual level – relationships between individuals within families and friendships.
2. Group level – networks within and between neighbourhoods, community organisations and groups.
3. Community and/or institutional level – the accumulation of individual and group relationships together with interaction between sub-communities and broad community sectors. This would also include the norms embedded in public organisations and societal institutions.
4. State or National Level – the cumulative total of networks, norms and trust across regions, states or even nations.

For example, conclusions made about social capital in regional towns (such as in Bullen and Onyx, 2003; Plowman et. al., 2003; Woolcock et. al., 2004) involve measurements of the mosaic of relationships and trust between individuals, families, and groups, together with people's broader perceptions of society. OECD (2001b) supports this concept of levels, identifying families, communities, firms and nations as sources of social capital.

Confounding
Social capital can be confounded with the existing social and economic well-being of communities. Residents of communities of high social capital may have the ability to build relationships and functional organisations, further building networks and trust. Indeed, Putnam (1993a) made the argument for self-reinforcing cycles of interaction that allowed social capital to build on itself.

The confounding question becomes far less clear when considering economic status. The confounding argument would say that more wealthy communities have the resources to organise and cooperate, and poor communities don't. Putnam (1993b) concluded that there was indeed an association between social capital and economic wellbeing in the rich north and poor south of

Italy. Berry et al. (1993) found that the limited resources of minorities and the poor restricted the representation of citizens in neighbourhood organisations.

Yet, social capital appears to have more to do with power and participation than financial resources. There are many examples of poor communities that have become remarkably empowered and built high levels of social capital (Piven and Cloward, 1979; Perry, 1987; Freire, 1973; Hollnsteiner, 1979; Gilbert, 1987).

'Hard' outcomes

Social capital is not just a matter of having stronger networks and 'soft' outcomes. It can lead to 'hard' outcomes such as improved community infrastructure, employment and services. In turn, better facilities and economic prospects can foster social interaction, confidence and community organisation.

Social capital can contribute to economic outcomes in a range of ways:
- reducing costs, e.g. Neighbourhood Watch can reduce policing costs;
- increasing production, e.g. a person starting a business relies on networks and contacts to establish a clientele and supply chains;
- increased efficiency, e.g. individuals or companies sharing inputs or marketing cooperatively;
- transfer of information and knowledge, e.g. better decisions from greater sharing of information and innovation;
- external benefits, e.g. health benefits of people being involved in their community.

Productivity Commission (2003) describe a range of economic and social outcomes of social capital including education and child welfare, government efficacy, health, crime reduction and economic performance. OECD (2001b) outline economic benefits such as increased productivity of firms, more effective production units, access to employment and regional innovation. However, macro-economic benefits from social capital were less clear.

A word of caution here. Social capital is a component of a broad process of change in communities and will not, of itself, overcome fundamental disadvantages in communities. A much broader realignment of power, opportunity and social change is required. Evidence also shows that effects are localised. It may be inappropriate to expect investment in social capital to have wide societal benefits.

Deficit model

Social capital requires a broader holistic understanding of community dynamics rather than a deficit/needs approach. Traditionally, service delivery has been based on a needs or deficit model. Applying a similar model to social capital may lead to inappropriate benchmarks for social capital and a focus on intervention to 'improve' low social capital.

This raises two apparent risks. First, there is a risk that conclusions can be based on an overall measure of social capital for a community, which can mask a great deal of variation and community dynamics. A second risk is assuming that deficits in social capital should be improved almost independently of community goals and ownership. Networks and relationships in different communities and groups may well be at different points with little ownership or motivation for improving social capital.

Cultural change

Social capital requires different assumptions and approaches beyond service delivery. This involves a cultural change where government, business and communities see social capital as 'core work', and where a community-strengthening agenda is more fully 'owned'. At present, the conceptual understanding of social capital outstrips the practical consideration of it in government, business and communities. Because social capital is difficult to measure (and understand) it is often seen as less important than bricks and mortar (Craig, 2002). Many agencies also continue to address social capital using the assumptions of service delivery and struggle to see its relevance to core business. This cultural change will require 'champions' in the rank and file of government, business and communities; repeated affirmation by key leaders; and 'real world' demonstrations of social capital and its benefits.

Value judgements

Social capital involves value judgements, rather than absolute truths. For example, anecdotally there is some evidence of people relocating to relatively prosperous coastal areas and not engaging in the local community. A major reason appears to be personal motivation and active disengagement from communities. Can this individual choice be described as poor or undesirable? Is it weak social capital, or is it simply the values and goals of a sector of the community? Clearly community engagement and social networks are desirable values in communities. However, to suggest that people should be involved in their community, and should build networks and participate, is nonetheless a value judgement.

Measurement of social capital

Social capital requires a different approach from traditional measures of performance. Yet many of the principles of traditional evaluation still apply. Many frameworks for the measurement of social capital and community well-being have been developed. Some common themes from this wide variety of approaches are:

- the use of both qualitative and quantitative data and a mix of techniques;
- measures of the cognitive elements of social capital (attitudes, norms and trust) and the 'structural' elements (networks, roles, organisation);
- community members are a key source of information;
- goal-oriented measurement involves evaluating changes in social capital resulting from a project or intervention. Absolute measurement involves assessing levels of social capital and community well-being regardless of particular activities.

The logic of social capital measurement in the frameworks above generally follows the generic logic of evaluation as follows:

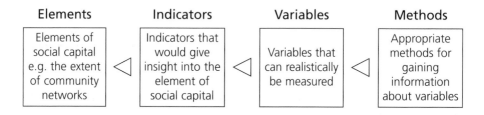

Elements	Indicators	Variables	Methods
Elements of social capital e.g. the extent of community networks	Indicators that would give insight into the element of social capital	Variables that can realistically be measured	Appropriate methods for gaining information about variables

The context and purpose of measurement

The context and purpose of social capital measurement is crucial to its measurement. There are several aspects to this, as follows:

1. There is tension in developing measures for social capital and the broader issue of why social capital is the way it is. What insight can be gained into what makes social capital 'work' in a particular community? Can measurement give insight into why networks are strong or weak or how participation is encouraged or discouraged?
2. Measurement requires a clear purpose. This will largely determine the nature of criteria to be measured, indicators and methods.

3. There is a risk of having comprehensive measurement but not having the assumptions and processes to interpret and act on the information. How do policy makers and practitioners respond to social capital issues identified by measurement? Do governments and communities have the policy, service delivery or community building responses, or ways to develop them?
4. Assessing social capital is not just a matter of measuring outputs, but also supporting local deliberation, decision making and planning.

Service delivery context

A service delivery culture has largely driven a high level of interest in evaluation and performance measurement. Yet, it brings with it assumptions that do not necessarily suit the measurement of social capital. The evaluation of service delivery is largely based on measuring clear inputs and outputs, has a focus on quantitative information, has quite specific performance indicators and measures change over a relatively short time period (often based on funding cycles). In contrast, the measurement of community change and social capital attempts to assess relatively ill-defined outcomes based on flexible processes. It relies on largely qualitative information with differences seen over long periods of time.

Moreover, while a lot of effort has gone into developing rigorous and accurate indicators, there is a risk that they will be interpreted using the assumptions of service delivery. These assumptions could easily create inappropriate conclusions, such as, if social capital has not changed after an intervention, then the intervention could be deemed unsuccessful, when longer-term changes are indeed happening.

Issues in evaluation
Isolating effects

Many factors influence the social situation of communities. Where possible, the effect of activities on social capital needs to be isolated from other effects. For example, feedback from community members can be focused on the extent to which community changes were due to a particular activity, rather than other influences.

The moving baseline

The starting point for activities aimed at fostering social capital is often taken to be the benchmark for comparison to measure impacts on social capital. However, the real comparison is against not what social capital was at the start, but against what social capital would have been if no intervention had occurred. It is clearly very difficult to measure this future 'without intervention' baseline but it needs to be considered in the interpretation of social capital impacts.

Direct and indirect effects

Changes to networks, norms and trust are likely to occur first within particular sectors of the community directly involved in community building activities. Broader community impacts are likely to occur indirectly as networks flow from these groups and cultural change gradually occurs. Hence measured changes are likely to be different between those directly affected and community members involved more indirectly.

Community involvement

In many circumstances it is appropriate for community members themselves to be engaged in the measurement of social capital. Measurement can be a social capital building exercise in itself with community members reflecting on how their community has changed.

Timeframe

Changes in social capital often involve long-term cultural change. Yet, in many cases, the timeframe for measurement is determined by funding arrangements or project timelines often with a timeframe of one to two years. In this timeframe, there may only be minor changes in networks, attitudes and trust. A longer-term approach needs to be incorporated into evaluation frameworks to assess more fundamental changes.

Data measurement and management

A range of methods have been developed to measure aspects of social capital. Yet there are several data measurement issues, for example:

1. Many indicators of social capital are not independent. That is, if you measure one indicator, such as people's participation in the community, you partly measure another indicator, such as people's networks and contacts. This limits the statistical analysis of data.
2. If a social capital variable can be triangulated by being measured in at least two ways, such as by verbal feedback and a Likert scale score, then the reliability of the information can be enhanced.

Benchmarks vs. incremental

A common way to measure social capital has been to benchmark criteria (Craig, 2002; Salvaris et al., 2000). That is, measure indicators at one point in time and measure the same criteria at another time and compare the two. Another way of measuring social capital is to assess incremental change. Rather than establishing an absolute benchmark, incremental change measures the change in social capital that has occurred over time, for example, how networks and trust have changed between now and this time last year.

Indicators

The measurement of social capital has featured the development of a wide range of indicators. There is also considerable interest in agreed local, state and national frameworks, and consistent indicators. Based on OECD (2001b), some key characteristics that guide the choice of indicators are:
- specificity – targeted to the variable to be measured;
- measurability – ease of measurement;
- comprehensiveness – measures of a range of social characteristics;
- reliability and rigour.

The challenge is to develop consistent indicators that can allow conclusions to be drawn across local, state and national frameworks. They need to have the flexibility to incorporate local values and what community members may want to measure. One way to achieve this compromise is to have local indicators as subsets of a more comprehensive set of State or national indicators. Given the complexity of social capital, it is not a matter of 'discovering' ideal indicators of social capital. Rather, measurement involves using often imperfect indicators and developing the confidence to work with inherent imperfections and uncertainty.

The contribution of evaluation to social capital

Evaluation can be a social capital building exercise in itself. The measurement of social capital can help community members rethink local issues, make better planning decisions and build ongoing community cohesion. Measurement can also be part of a cultural change process allowing government and business to better appreciate and incorporate social capital.

Conclusion

Despite considerable knowledge of social capital and developing measurement to the point of developing State and national frameworks, many questions about why remain. Why does social capital operate the way it does? Why do different sectors of communities have such different social capital characteristics? Why do networks and norms change in the way they do?

The challenge for measurement is not only to develop consistent rigorous ways to assess social capital but to also provide further insight into these questions.

Chapter 4

Community, the State and social capital impact assessment

Martin Mowbray
Emeritus Professor, RMIT University, Australia

Introduction

In this chapter, I challenge the orthodox, localist approach to the concept of social capital generally applied by politicians and governments. This is the school of thought led by Harvard University Professor Robert Putnam. Contrary to the thrust of the dominant Putnamian perspective, I argue that the concept of social capital in public policy should be understood more as a function of the broad range of state policies, rather than as an effect of the very limited interventions at local level – often styled as community building.

Because orthodox approaches mostly fail to explain or contextualise their particular perspective on social capital it is necessary to begin with a brief review of its rise to prominence. Along with setting out its main features, I note the way in which political leaders eagerly embrace Putnam's thesis. By focusing on consensual community building programmes as the prime means for generating social capital, government agencies divert attention from the implications of more substantial forces and policies, especially those operating at macro levels such as in economic change and management. They also do this by restricting their interest to only some narrow aspects of the measurement of social capital.

The point of pursuing this is that there is generally too little interest in assessing how wider state policies affect social capital. For the concept of social capital to merit more serious attention in public policy, the idea of social impact assessment, relatively undeveloped to this point, should be pursued.

'the man with the Big Idea ... "social capital"'

When a prominent Australian journalist (Grattan, 2003) wrote about 'the man with the Big Idea ... "social capital"' she meant Peter Costello, the Treasurer in the conservative Australian federal government. However, her words best fit Robert Putnam. Putnam is the figure who has done most to elaborate on the concept of 'social capital', having first brought his ideas about social capital to public attention in trying to account for the social, political and economic differences between the north and south of Italy. Social capital was his key explanatory concept. However, Putnam's 'big idea' was not original. Its conceptual roots lie considerably earlier and in more diverse places than Putnam acknowledges (Farr, 2004).

Through prescience and opportunism, or just fortune, Putnam adopted and embellished a notion with astonishing political and policy resonance. Thanks to Putnam, influential intellectuals who shape public agendas and policy makers inherited a very appealing concept with substantial data already aimed at topical problems in the fields of health, education, employment, crime, security and welfare. Most alluring to policy makers was the thrift of the associated line of attack. According to the Putnam stratagem, a focus on creating social capital would not be expensive for government.

Aided by such lure, there may be no other academic term that has had such a meteoric rise. Like an escaped laboratory virus, 'social capital' swiftly 'spread from Harvard's school of government to the think-tank world, and then to politicians, civil servants and beyond' (Rogers, 2003). This observation is particularly pertinent in Australia, where Putnam's claims first came to public attention through the periodical of the country's oldest free-market think-tank, the Institute of Public Affairs. In that article, Putnam employed one of his signature generalisations: that 'communities don't have choral societies because they are wealthy; they are wealthy because they have choral societies' (1994, p. 34). By this, Putnam meant that northern Italy was richer than the south as a result of having a greater store of social capital, demonstrated through historically higher levels of associational membership. It was not, as his critics have charged, a result of colonisation and state building (Tarrow, 1996) or of political struggle (Navarro, 2002).

The declining social capital thesis strongly corresponds with the longstanding notion of a community lost. As Raymond Williams demonstrated in *The Country and the City* (1975) this idea of a happier and more communal way of life before the advent of modern social problems has deep cultural and literary roots. Into the established attraction of the idea of a vanishing community, Putnam injects a strong alarmist element; what O'Hara (2004, p. 281) terms a 'narrative of doom'. Putnam's fame and influence mostly arises from the argument that over the last 40 years, civic life in the US has declined to such an extent as to threaten the economic and social well-being of the nation.

The initial surge to prominence of this 'neo-Tocquevillean' (Putnam, 1995, p. 66)[1] idea came with his 1995 paper 'Bowling alone: America's declining social capital'. Very soon one commentator was able to write that this 'slender article ... spawned more commentary than *Hamlet*' (Pollitt, 1996) and another that:

> Seldom has a thesis moved so quickly from scholarly obscurity to conventional wisdom. By January 1996 the *Washington Post* was featuring a six part series of front-page articles on the decline of trust. (Galston, 1996)

Putnam himself evocatively acknowledges that, having published 'scores of books' that had not 'attracted the slightest public attention', he remained obscure until publishing 'Bowling alone'. Then he was 'invited to Camp David, lionized by talk-show hosts' and pictured on the front page of *People* (Putnam, 2000, p. 506).

This was despite what he admits was 'limited evidence' in need of confirmation (Putnam, 1995, p. 67; 2000, p. 506). Putnam's declining social capital thesis was a worldwide hit before he published his bestseller on the topic. Also called *Bowling Alone*, it is probably the most popular social science monograph, at least for its policy impact. Reviewers (see Putnam, 2000, pp. 1–3) declare that its significance rivals classics such as *The Lonely Crowd* (David Riesman, 1950), *The Power Elite* (C. Wright Mills, 1956) and *The Affluent Society* (J.K. Galbraith, 1958).

In 2003, with co-author Lewis Feldstein, Putnam followed *Bowling Alone* with a book of case studies about how to recreate stocks of social capital through community building. It is most unlikely that any other book concerning community development was ever greeted with as much fanfare as Putnam and Feldstein's *Better Together*. As one US columnist wrote a few months after publication:

> Feldstein has been travelling the nation giving talks to crowds as large as 500 in Seattle and 300 in Chicago, sometimes on his own,

sometimes with Putnam ... The book tour is going 'superbly', Feldstein said ... 'the book has crossed over into being a news story, as the subject of lead edits (editorials) in a number of papers: the *San Francisco Chronicle*, the Portland *Oregonian*, the *Santa Clara Union*'. (Charpentier, 2003)

Though dispute over the accuracy and adequacy of Putnam's evidence about declining civic engagement flared in isolated parts of academia, such controversy is rare (Galston, 1996). This is despite often-indiscriminate projection of claims about the US to other societies, including in Europe, Australia and developing nations. A remarkable and instructive feature of the orthodox usage of social capital is the customary disregard for the many damning criticisms of Putnam's approach (for example, Skocpol, 1996; Fine, 2001; Harriss, 2002; Mayer, 2003; Muntaner and Lynch, 2002; Schuurman, 2003).

Evidence of the pandemic 'social capital movement' (Putnam, 2000, p. 510) is easily found. On the Internet a hub of social capital websites, Capitale Sociale[2], links 35 other sites. These include those of the World Bank, the OECD, Harvard's BetterTogether, and the Australian Bureau of Statistics' 'Social Capital Theme Page'.

Putnam's thesis

Essential features of Putnam's thesis centre on his particular definition, the causes and implications of declining social capital, and what should be done.

Definition

For Putnam 'social capital refers to connections among individuals – social networks and the norms of reciprocity and trustworthiness that arise from them' (Putnam, 1994, p. 34; 2000, p. 19). In the wider Putnamian usage, 'social glue' is a synonym for social capital. Putnam also uses various other synonyms such as social cohesion, social connectedness and even fraternity (Putnam, 2000, pp. 326–9, 351). Terms incorporating the word 'together' are closely associated and emblematic, as in *Better Together* (Putnam and Feldstein, 2003) and the BetterTogether website.[3]

Others such as French sociologist Pierre Bourdieu (1930–2002) have used 'social capital' in contrasting ways. Rather than seeing social capital as an integrative or cohesive resource, Bourdieu employed the term to help explain the perpetuation of class and the differential distribution of power, privilege and economic domination. Clearly, Putnam's approach with its emphasis on togetherness is more useful for those who prefer to overlook or downplay fundamental conflicts of interests in social institutions, localities or nations (Siisiäinen, 2000, p. 23). Assisting this, the Putnam definition is usually taken as the only one, and sometimes the impression is given that Putnam actually coined the term (for example, Giddens, 1999).

For Putnam, social capital can take very tangible forms, such as volunteer ambulance squads, bridge clubs and Rotary clubs (2000, p. 21). He also refers to religious communities as 'very important repositories of social capital' (Putnam and Feldstein, 2003, p. 120). The 'most fundamental form of social capital is the family' (Putnam, 1995, p. 73). In contrast, Putnam does not regard organisations such as Greenpeace as manifesting social capital. Peculiarly, this is partly because he sees their 'direct mail recruits' as holding 'more extreme and intolerant political views' than members of organisations recruited through social networks (2000, p. 158).

Causes

Putnam identifies the main culprits for declining social capital and estimates their relative contributions to its decline. These are: first, 'pressures of time and money' – 10 per cent; second, urban sprawl – 10 per cent; third, electronic entertainment, especially television – 25 per cent; fourth, and most importantly, the replacement of the 'unusually civic generation', whose 'social habits and values' were substantially shaped by World War II and by several (post-civic) generations … less embedded in community life' – 50 per cent (Putnam, 2000, pp. 255, 275, 283). This blame accompanies Putnam's cursory exoneration of the state, business and the market (Putnam, 2000, pp. 279–83).

'So what?'[4]

Putnam contends that social capital has declined to such an extent as to endanger a way-of-life. The 'civic-minded trends that characterized the first two thirds of the twentieth century' have reversed (Putnam, 2000, pp. 180–4).

According to Putnam, this matters because social capital can reduce transaction costs, and 'society that relies on generalized reciprocity is more efficient than a distrustful society' (Putnam, 2000, p. 135). '[W]here trust and social networks flourish individuals, firms, neighbourhoods, and even nations prosper' (Putnam, 2000, p. 319). Later, adding a nationalist theme to the economic, he writes 'economies whose citizens have … high social capital – will dominate the twenty-first century' (Putnam, 2000, p. 325).

In addition, Putnam points to numerous personal benefits from higher levels of social capital, ranging from greater happiness, better health, higher income and levels of educational achievement, to lower rates of child abuse and other crimes against person. Putnam casts many of his claims flamboyantly, in what he calls 'stylized generalizations' (Putnam, 2000, p. 399). For example, social capital goes with family life (Putnam, 2000, p. 278) and 'in round numbers, getting married is the "happiness equivalent" of quadrupling your annual income' (Putnam, 2000, p. 333). Putnam loosely cites an Atlanta finding 'that each employed person in one's social network increases one's annual income by US$1,400' (Putnam, 2000, p. 322).

A third example, with equal disregard for the crucial distinction between causation and association and the problem of inferring from aggregate data to individuals, is one adopted by policy-makers as true for the state of Victoria:

> As a rough rule of thumb, if you belong to no groups but decide to join one, you cut your risk of dying over the next year in half. If you smoke and belong to no groups, it's a toss-up statistically whether you should stop smoking or start joining. (Putnam, 2000, p. 331; Moodie, 2003; Delahunty, 2003; Pike, 2003)

'Possible therapies' or 'what is to be done'[5]

The final element in Putnam's thesis concerns his answer to the question 'what is to be done?' Putnam concludes *Bowling Alone* with the chapter 'Towards an agenda for social capitalists'. The central message is that US citizens should all resolve to participate more 'not because it will be good for America – though it will be – but because it will be good for us' (2000, p. 414). Essentially, Putnam's message is for citizens. He urges 'government officials, political consultants, politicians and (above all)' citizens 'to find ways to ensure that by 2010 many more Americans will participate in the public life of our communities' (Putnam, 2000, p. 412).

'Nothing could be safer than a speech about social capital'

In mid-2003, social capital hit the Australian headlines when the Treasurer, Peter Costello, moved tactically to affirm his own aptitude for Prime Ministerial office. Keen to parade his more human qualities, Costello said he would speak out on issues beyond the economic (McMurray, 2003). Through a newspaper column 'Costello, the social capitalist', Michelle Grattan wrote that Costello saw 'the social capital idea' as a means by which he could appear innovative and progressive – 'to dance around the floor, nimble on his feet, touching the shoes of a few colleagues without treading on them'. Another columnist, Adele Horin, described Costello's speeches, as not simply politically conservative, but cynical. 'Is there anything easier in politics than to praise a volunteer? Is there anything safer than to exhort people to get involved in their communities?' (Horin, 2003).

In addresses to a national welfare agency (Costello, 2003a) and to a conservative think-tank (Costello, 2003b) Costello expounded his newfound enthusiasm about social capital and the need to restore our lost community. In the absence of appropriate Australian research, Costello said that 'all the anecdotal evidence' he had gathered confirmed what Putnam reported in *Bowling Alone* – 'social capital is running down' (Costello, 2003b). On one hand, Costello's approach entailed repeated reference to trust, tolerance, voluntary association, charity and mutual obligation. On the other, and pointedly juxtaposed, he reiterated the importance of a residual state. Costello accentuated his point that building social capital is a duty that lies 'outside government'. Government, he insisted, had the residual responsibility to 'do no harm'.

Media interest in social capital escalated. Anxious to share the political kudos associated with the invocation of 'social capital', a stream of other Australian politicians then jostled to associate themselves with the idea (Mowbray, 2004a).

Government and social capital

Robert Putnam's view is that social capital's 'conceptual cousin' is 'community' (Putnam, 2000, p. 21) and that community building is the operational dimension of social capital. The Secretary of the Department for Victorian Communities reports the Victorian Government's approach on how to increase social capital in plain and frank terms:

> The role for government in generating social capital is to create the opportunities for individuals to establish relationships and shared values; that is, to facilitate the creation of networks. The site for network creation is the local community, and community strengthening is the means to do so. (Blacher, 2003)

In other words, the government's job is to assist individual citizens in their local environments to form relationships and shape mutual values. Later in the same report (p. 9) the Department for Victorian Communities tells us that 'increasingly, community strengthening strategies are being understood in terms of their role in building social capital'.

As noted above Robert Putnam bases his strategy for change on a call to citizens to participate more at the local level. In the Putnamian view there is nothing basically wrong with existing political and economic arrangements. No redistribution of power or access to resources is necessary. Nor are race, ethnic and gender relations in need of significant change. Similarly, international affairs are unproblematic or even irrelevant to social capital.

This position is well demonstrated in the book *Better Together* (Putnam and Feldstein, 2003), 'the hopeful flip side of *Bowling Alone*' (Charpentier, 2003). Funded by many philanthropic funds, including the Ford and Rockefeller Foundation, and the Carnegie Corporation, *Better Together* is an uncritical commendation of community building as the key means for effecting social change. Twelve very lightly researched but wholly triumphant case studies of projects with more or less participatory dimensions make up each of the book's chapters, bordered by an introduction and conclusion.

In their conclusion Putnam and Feldstein note that the 'case studies focus on the actions in the foreground, not the structural conditions in the background' (Putnam and Feldstein, 2003, p. 271). And they are almost totally devoid of material about advocacy. *Better Together*'s case studies are of the 'consensus organising' variety, so much favoured in government-sponsored community-building programmes (see Mowbray, 2004b).

It is indeed odd that references to wider social advocacy are absent from the case studies, especially considering that they are intended as a guide to the 'broader revival of social capital' (Putnam and Feldstein, 2003, p. 5). Advocacy as an activity only appears in the occasional reference to very low-key and localised examples, such as where a group of schoolchildren manage to convince authorities to make a railway crossing safer by installing warning lights (Putnam and Feldstein, 2003, p. 142).

Though Putnam and Feldstein clearly acknowledge that the role of the state is also critical (Putnam and Feldstein, 2003, pp. 271–5), this caveat appears as an afterthought. Putnam and Feldstein choose each case to make the pre-conceived point that 'the community can do it'. The selected cases are meant to further the general thesis that effectively organised communities can resolve the problems or challenges that confront them, and everyone benefits. Politics is not an issue and readers see little sign of disagreement or difference, let alone debate. The overwhelming flavour is of consensus. The claim that 'social capital is necessarily a local phenomenon' and generally formed 'through local personal contact' (Putnam and Feldstein, 2003, p. 9) is another embedded theme.

What else may determine levels of social capital?

Complementing the passing caveat that civil society alone cannot solve public issues, Putnam and Feldstein (2003, p. 273) offer other observations on how social capital is otherwise affected. One of these, also noted in passing, is that 'misguided public policies can weaken or destroy social capital' (2003, p. 273). For the Putnam school, and those others who prefer to see social capital as a function of community level activity, this point is a potential source of trouble. It is a Pandora's box that should be opened if the conservative 'government must do no harm' principle is to be taken seriously. This is also the case if we heed another of Putnam's caveats that appears to contradict the idea that social capital is itself causal. This is that social capital is, in part, a consequence of public policy (Putnam, 2001).

In pursuing the issue of what caused the decay of civic engagement, Putnam raises a corresponding issue. This is that governments may also do things that though not necessarily meant to influence social capital, nevertheless do so in powerful ways. Deciding on war is an obvious example. Putnam's analysis of the role of the Second World War in the USA leads him to point out the 'practical implication' of finding 'the moral equivalent of war'[6] for civic renewal (Putnam, 2000, p. 276). Not anticipating events such as those of 11 September 2001, he warily ventured:

> Creating (or recreating) social capital is no simple task. It would be eased by a palpable national crisis, like war or depression or national disaster, but for better and for worse, America at the dawn of the new century faces no such galvanizing crisis. (Putnam, 2000, p. 402)

Quite obviously, many types of policies apart from war will critically influence issues central to the Putnamian conceptualisation of social capital. Government policies that bear on the distribution of wealth (including land) and income, opportunity and influence – political accountability, public infrastructure and access to services, corporate greed, the integrity of the criminal justice system, and international relations – are all likely to affect levels of societal trust and social cohesion.

Inequality and social capital

Putnam explicitly associates the decline of civic engagement with a declining level of economic equality. The high point in civic connectedness, he argues, was in the 1950s and 1960s, when the USA was 'more egalitarian than it had been in more than a century'. 'Sometime around 1965–70 America reversed course and started becoming both less just economically and less well connected socially and politically' (Putnam, 2000, p. 359). This is a crucial but neglected hypothesis about what most affects social capital, one supported by many others.

Johnson, Headey and Jensen (2003, p. 38), for example, cite 'fairly strong evidence, both at national and local levels, that rates of civic participation are greater in places with higher and more equal incomes'. They also report that participation – particularly political participation – is highest of all in the West's most egalitarian countries: Sweden, Norway, Denmark and the Netherlands. A British study suggests that a post-war drop in trust is coincident with 'sharply growing inequality' and the 'changing nature of working life' (Grenier and Wright, 2003, p. 24).

Kawachi, Kennedy and Lochner (1997) report a positive correlation between levels of cohesiveness and economic inequality. They suggest that rising income inequalities are associated with declining trust and that an 'egalitarian distribution of wealth and income seems to imply a more cohesive, harmonious society' (p. 58). They relate this to government policy which, 'in recent years … has tended to reinforce growing inequality'. This leads seamlessly into the association between economic inequality, social capital and health, a theme deeply entrenched in the health literature, as Hawe and Shiell (2000) and Szreter and Woolcock (2002) demonstrate in their detailed reviews.

In Australia, the Victorian State Minister of Health recognised this associa-tion, drawing attention to the implications for health services of the 'widening gap in income levels in Australia'. Similarly, she reports that 'death rates tend to be higher in countries and regions where income differences between the rich and poor are larger'. Tellingly, the Minister says, the 'sharp end comes', 'when we ask how we can make use of this information'. Predictably, the Minister quickly retreated and plumped for a communitarian approach. Her risk-free and anodyne conclusion is that at least until 'all the important factors in determining people's health' are better understood she backs the value of building community and togetherness as the most efficacious solution (Pike, 2003, p. 9).

Carson suggests that this sort of political deflection of responsibility from the state to 'non-governmental collectivities and individuals' is not far from 'blaming the community for its own woes' (Carson, 2004, pp. 15, 17). Alcock makes a similar point, as well as drawing attention to the argument from urban sociology that concentration on area-based explanations of problems obscures their 'fundamentally structural' origins (Alcock, 2004, pp. 93–4). Fairly obviously, government policies that affect the distribution of income are likely to have a far greater impact on social capital than low-budget, short-term, localised and fragmented community building programmes located at the margins of government.

More fundamental to the question about the genuineness of government commitment to enhancing social capital is its interest in assessing the ramifications of its policies. Though there is distinct interest on the part of government in measuring social capital (for example, ABS, 2004) and its association with issues such as health (for example, Cullen and Whiteford, 2001), there is no commensurate concern for assessing the impacts of government policies on social capital.

Measuring government impacts on social capital

In the ocean of literature on measuring levels of social capital, an extremely small proportion deals with the problem of policy outcomes, other than limited evaluations of community-building programmes. However, some writers clearly recognise the issue. In her nationally broadcast (Boyer) lectures in 1995, Eva Cox advocated development of a social capital impact statement[7] before governments sold public assets (Cox, 1995, pp. 77–8).

Towards the end of *Bowling Alone*, Putnam also fleetingly suggests that new government programmes be preceded by social capital impact statements 'calling attention to unanticipated consequences' (Putnam, 2000, p. 413; see also 1995, p. 76). The kinds of programmes Putnam had in mind were about urban renewal or freeways.

Cox and Caldwell have usefully extended the application of 'social capital accounting' to specific policies. Policies should be 'assessed for their likely impact on trust and community cohesion'. They provide a list of 'initial questions' for such assessment. These are generally about the way in which people experience certain policies. How, for example, would they affect social skills, values and attitudes? (Cox and Caldwell, 2000, pp. 68–70).

The Australian Productivity Commission takes Cox and Caldwell's 'checklist' slightly further, but in a conservative direction. It provides a list of government policies with possible side effects on social capital. These include, for example, 'certain labour market policies' which allegedly 'price unemployed people out of jobs'; or welfare payments which may 'reduce incentives to work, create dependency and displace private charity, thus harming social capital' (Productivity Commission, 2003, section 4.2).

Tellingly, the Productivity Commission generally confines its discussion to the realm of social policy, and categorically avoids other politically divisive policy fields such as corporate accountability, economic policies that directly affect the distribution of income and wealth, or the place of Aboriginal people in Australian society. Predictably, the Australian Bureau of Statistics (ABS) provides a similarly conservative account of social capital. Indigenous people are unseen and the sweep of the literature fails to deal with divergent and troublesome viewpoints (ABS, 2004).

Though its intervention is ostensibly about measurement of social capital, the ABS also manages to overlook a fundamental issue that the Productivity Commission does raise. This is measuring the impacts on social capital of government policies. The ABS says that measurement of social capital is required for three purposes: establishing (1) national and sub-national social capital profiles or benchmarks; (2) the effects of social capital on well-being, (such as health, employment and education); and (3) the success of projects meant to 'nurture' social capital. (ABS, 2004, p. 11).

The ABS provides a list of examples of government 'programmes involving social capital' across Australia. Most of these are local or community-building type programmes and all fall within the realms of social and health policy. None concern governments' major policy portfolios that deal with the economy and business, criminal justice, transport and communications, the environment, or international relations (ABS, 2004, p. 10).

The ABS then lists a selection of 'government surveys with questions relating to social capital'. Again, all of these fall within the realms of social and health policy (ABS, 2004, p. 11). Here again, we have an example of a government agency expounding on the virtue and importance of social capital, but declining to recognise most of the administrative and policy domains likely to have the greatest influence on social capital.

Conclusion: towards social capital impact assessment

Most public policy concerning social capital is generally in line with the approach of Robert Putnam. However, many of Putnam's reservations or caveats are overlooked, often expediently. Alternative definitions of social capital are also generally ignored, as are the numerous problems with Putnam's approach identified by its critics. So that social capital can be presented as a totally positive phenomenon, even the negative aspects of social capital, labelled by Putnam as the 'dark side', are mostly unacknowledged.

Responsibility for the maintenance or protection of social capital is largely seen as a matter for civil society or community, making it easier to insinuate or conclude that the origins of problems are also localised. The role of the state is generally portrayed as residual, and facilitative at most. The chief means for strengthening social capital is presented as being in the realm of social policy, especially through family support or community-(re)building schemes. Moreover, these typically have an integrative and consensual character. Finally, while there is pronounced government interest in measuring levels of social capital, this is in 'snapshots' or in the effects of community building interventions of limited scope, time and resources. There is virtually no government interest in assessing the ways in which wider state policies might affect social capital, negatively or positively, for better or for worse.

The literature on social capital is immense, and almost certainly some of its innumerable contributors have elaborated a more satisfactory approach to assessing the impacts of policies on forms of social capital than I have been able to locate. In any case, there is no reason why some of the more flexible and penetrating tools for unravelling public policy, such as that of David Gil (1992), could not be readily adapted for assessing policy impacts on social capital. The fundamental point is, however, that governments are reluctant to examine the impact on social capital of their most important policies, such as those that affect the distribution of income.

Despite widespread expressions of concern about trustworthiness in government, politicians are reluctant to encourage careful analysis or auditing of the relevant effects of their policies. This paradox is, according to an analysis of post-war UK polls, accompanied by another; 'perceived trust-worthiness rarely swings an election' (O'Hara, 2004, p. 274).

While there is much that is problematic with the notion of social capital, it is now well established. Social capital is currently a vogue concept with a good deal of momentum in public policy. The challenge to policy-makers, generally avoided, is to put it to as good a use as possible. One such means is for the concept of social capital, or variations on it like trust, to be applied in shedding more light on the often-unseen implications of government policies.

To demonstrate their genuine and often repeated concern about levels of social capital, we should demand that policy makers assiduously assess the impact on social capital of all major policies, explicit and implicit. To verify their often-professed interest or commitment to the importance of the concept, governments should, as a matter of course, enable independent and wholehearted public analysis of the effects of all policies with a potentially significant effect on social capital, or its associated concepts such as social cohesion or public trust. Such analysis might be termed social capital impact assessment, though the name is unimportant. Amongst other things, the process should take into account policies that, however indirectly, affect the distribution of income and wealth; access to opportunity including health, education and employment; the integrity of the criminal justice system; race, ethnic and gender relations; and corporate behaviour.

Moreover, there is no reason why, in the absence of cooperation, governments should not conduct or sponsor such assessments of the impacts of other governments. These would range across formal jurisdictional boundaries, municipal and regional, federal and international.

Notes

[1] Putnam refers to the French political scientist Alexis de Tocqueville's 1830s observation that 'Americans' propensity for civic association' was the 'key to their unprecedented ability to make democracy work'. Putnam labels analysts who point to the effect of civic or community engagement on social, economic and governmental variables, Neo-Tocquevilleans (Putnam, 1995, p. 66).

[2] Capitale Sociale, University of Rome. http://w3.uniroma1.it/soccap/eng-websitessocialcapital.htm.

[3] BetterTogether website. http://bettertogether.org/.

[4] Putnam's title for Section 4 of *Bowling Alone* on the consequences of social capital.

[5] Putnam's term for approaches to renewal of 'civic engagement and social connectedness', set out in Section 5 of *Bowling Alone* (Putnam, 2000, p. 28).

[6] 'The moral equivalent of war' is the title of William James' 1906 essay about the challenge for the state of sustaining political cohesion without resorting to war-making. http://www.constitution.org/wj/meow.htm.

[7] Using Google (on 9 June 2004) I searched on 'social capital impact assessment' and 'social capital impact statement(s)' and found 10 and 31 results respectively, some overlapping. Given the immensity of the social capital literature, this seems to be a remarkably small number.

Chapter 5

Social networks, innovation and learning: can policies for social capital promote both dynamism and justice?

John Field

Deputy Principal (Research and External Relations), University of Stirling, Scotland

Learning, innovation and social capital are closely associated with one another. People who take part in community activities are more likely to be participating in learning, and organisations that have strong internal linkages are more likely to adopt new approaches to the way they conduct their business. Conversely, people who are pursuing new skills and knowledge are more likely to engage in civic life, and innovative organisations are likely to build and contribute to networks and clusters. It therefore seems sensible to conclude that networks and sociability are important ingredients in any coherent strategy to build a learning society and a sustainable economy. And since social capital can equally be shown to promote many other benefits for individuals and the community – from health improvements to reductions in crime levels – it seems that a good society must be one that promotes broad innovative capabilities with lifelong learning for all.

At first sight then, there seems to be a very clear and obvious message for policy makers. If social capital promotes learning, learning promotes social capital, and both help to promote other desirable goals, then policy measures should be adopted which support lifelong learning and build social capital. Yet of course things are rarely so simple in the complex world of policy. Some researchers have challenged the belief that social capital and lifelong learning are wedded comfortably and fruitfully together (St Clair, 2005). And even if it can be shown that the two are at least cheerful cohabitees, it does not follow that government can find and follow a simple menu of policy prescriptions for both lifelong learning and social capital are complex, ill-defined areas, populated by a vast array of poorly-coordinated actors with a variety of goals. If leaving things to the market is not an option, nor is a simple growth in public provision.

One of the reasons that policy is complex is that it is not clear that innovation, learning and social capital are readily compatible with social justice and equality. On the contrary; each may be pursued without any positive impact upon existing inequalities, and moreover they may well reinforce these inequalities or create new ones. Examples spring readily to mind. Thus the promotion of lifelong learning may inadvertently lead to the creation of a 'learning divide' between the 'knowledge rich' and 'knowledge poor', which in turn legitimates the exclusion of those who fail to acquire the required skills and credentials. Similarly, policies designed to promote community development may be iniquitous if disadvantaged groups and communities are isolated for some reason from networks and resources that are situated outside their own community.

This chapter reviews the nature of the relationship between innovation, learning and social capital, and then goes on to consider some of the implications for policy and practice. It starts by examining recent work on social capital and learning, and moves on to assess the debate on social capital and innovation. In each case, I acknowledge that there are significant 'dark sides' to the debate, as well as positive resources that can promote capabilities for sustainable growth and social justice. In reviewing the evidence, I also acknowledge that there is some force in certain scholarly criticisms of the current debates over social capital, innovation and learning; in particular, some research does not point to a clear and linear relationship between the various factors, but rather indicates much that is highly contingent. Nevertheless, I conclude that ducking the policy challenge is deeply conservative; however radical the language, it boils down to letting market forces take their course. Rather than lamenting the risks and threats of policy development, we should try to turn the debate on its head, and ask what policies might be adopted if we place sustainability and justice at the heart of our approach.

A virtuous cycle?

By far the best known writer on this topic is the American political scientist, Robert Putnam. Putnam, since the mid-90s, has been centrally preoccupied with what he believes is the collapse of community in the United States

(Putnam, 1995, 2000). Drawing on a massive reserve of survey data and membership records, Putnam famously demonstrated that civic connected-ness in the USA had declined dramatically since the 1950s. By comparing data cross the individual states, Putnam also showed that populations with the lowest levels of civic engagement were overwhelmingly likely to suffer from high crime rates, poor health, weak economic growth and wretched educa-tional attainment; conversely, populations with high levels of social capital enjoyed a much better quality of life (Putnam, 2000). While educational attainment, for Putnam, is simply one among many indicators of quality of life, his evidence clearly suggests a positive association between social capital and human capital.

This was, of course, not a new notion. The specific idea that human capital and social capital complement one another is rooted in James Coleman's work on schooling. Coleman led a major study for the United States Office of Education of school achievements among African American pupils in the 1960s, drawing on a monumental amount of data to demonstrate that although schools had a significant direct influence on pupil attainment, in certain circumstances it was outweighed by community and family characteristics (Coleman et al., 1966). Coleman explained this relationship with reference to social capital, which he defined as 'the set of resources that inhere in family relations and in the community social organisation and that are useful for the cognitive development of a child or young person' (Coleman, 1994, p. 300). More specifically, Coleman pointed to the dense ties that existed around faith-based schools, involving not only the school and its teachers but also the parents, the clergy and the wider community. Simply stated, social capital for Coleman 'exists in the interest, even the intrusiveness, of one adult in the activities of someone else's child' (Coleman, 1990, p. 334). While ties rooted in the immediacy of family were strongest of all, Coleman also took a bright view of organised religion as a basis for positive cooperation. He appears to have had no particular interest in the types of connectedness that fascinate Putnam, such as sports, volunteering or work-based socialising.

Further empirical work on ethnic minority communities in the USA and Europe has generally tended to support Coleman's central finding, of a positive association between social capital and pupil achievement. A North American meta-analysis of fourteen empirical studies found that the majority reported a positive association between different scores on both counts (Dika and Singh, 2002, pp. 41–3). European researchers (Lauglo, 2000) have provided further support. It has also been found that social connections, notably family ties, appear to play a significant role in promoting transitions to higher education, a role which is particularly important for middle-class school-leavers and mature students (Reay, David and Ball, 2005).

Precisely why educational attainment and social capital are so deeply intermeshed is not yet entirely clear, but their positive association with one another is well established. Coleman's initial suggestion was that the social-isation process was at its most powerful when all the key adult influences – parents, teachers, neighbours and priests – were singing in harmony (Coleman, 1990, 1994). Essentially, his argument focused on the positive pressures and negative sanctions that influenced young people's behaviour. However, a reading of Pierre Bourdieu's influential work on the role of cultural and social capital in reproducing social and economic inequalities suggests that there is more to it than simple pressures to conform to community norms (Bourdieu and Passeron, 1977; Bourdieu, 1980). There is a simple process of calling in favours: school children acquire connections through their school, often by proxy, who will intervene on their behalf (for example, a teacher who calls their old college tutor); this process almost invariably favours the relatively well-placed (Reay, David and Ball, 2005). And perhaps even more importantly, there are hidden cognitive gains from social connections. Family has been shown to influence such capacities as verbal facility and behavioural patterns, with evidence of serious cognitive disadvantages for children born into families where parents were unemployed or low-skilled (Parcel and Menaghan, 1994).

So far, the evidence reviewed has concerned social capital and learning among the young. In contrast with the relatively clear findings of Coleman and his successors, researchers in adult learning have produced rather complicated results. First, much research has found that, as with young people, many adults derive educational advantages from their social connections. Recent statistical analysis in Wales points to the persistent influence of family on participation in adult learning, with an impact that appears to stretch back at least three generations (Gorard and Rees, 2002). While this study is unusual in examining the role of family in adult learning, a well-established body of work points to a positive mutual relationship between active citizenship and adult learning. Internationally, an analysis of the International Adult Literacy Survey results for 17 countries showed a positive association between levels of participation in adult education on the one hand, and membership of voluntary associations (and, to a lesser extent, trust) on the other (Tuijnman and Boudard, 2001, p. 40). A similar comparison of data from the European Values Survey and the European Labour Force Survey produced similar results (Field, 2005, p. 36).

The most substantial body of evidence in the UK comes from an extensive study of volunteering and learning in the English Midlands (Elsdon, Reynolds and Stewart, 1995), which incidentally demonstrated that levels of volunteering – particularly in local and self-help bodies – were seriously understated by official statistics. This study's findings have been confirmed by work elsewhere in the UK. Thus in a small-scale study of adult learners on access courses, a type of programme that presupposes a significant commitment to personal development and formal study, Roseanne Benn found that two-thirds had previously been active in voluntary organisations (Benn, 1996).

Benn concluded that civic participation helped people develop valuable cognitive and affective resources, in particular a willingness to take risks and a stronger individual 'perception of power and self-worth' (Benn, 1996, p. 173). It is not clear from Benn's work whether all forms of participation produced these learning gains, but a study of adult learning in a northern French mining region in the 1970s suggested that it is important to distinguish between different types of participation. In this study, Charles Hedoux found that people who took part in traditional festivals and societies were no more likely to attend adult education than those who did not; however, people who engaged in more 'modern' forms of community life, which brought them into contact with 'local notables', were much more likely to be active learners (Hedoux, 1982, p. 264).

An analysis of British survey data also pointed to a differentiated pattern of association between civic engagement and adult learning; in general, participation in learning was higher among people involved in sociable and out-going forms of leisure and volunteering, and lower among people involved in home-based pursuits, such as gardening (Field, 2003b). A more detailed analysis of Northern Ireland survey data suggested a further degree of complexity (Field, 2005, pp. 88–96). In this study, levels of participation in learning were highest among those who were relatively active in named forms of civic engagement and lowest among those who were relatively inactive. However, there was a third group, consisting of those who were completely uninvolved in the named forms of civic engagement; they were less likely to be learning participants than were people who were active members of the community, but more likely to be learning than people who were occasionally active in the community. A simple model of joiners (with high levels of participation in learning) and non-joiners (with low levels of participation in learning) simply will not do.

So far, the analysis has concentrated on evidence pointing to a positive if complex association between social capital and adult learning. However, a small body of work poses questions about the universality of this pattern. In the case of Northern Ireland, some survey and qualitative data point to the possibility that, for many purposes (including such key transitions as job-finding), some people rely on connections instead of participating in formal learning (Field, 2005, pp. 40–62). It is important to emphasise that this did **not** mean that people were learning nothing at all; indeed, the prevalence of social connections as a source of information and ideas meant that much learning took place informally. But informal learning and social connections appeared to substitute for, rather than complement, participation in organised learning. This has a number of consequences, including a tendency for out-sider exclusion (so that information did not reach people who were not in key networks) and self-exclusion (as in communities who actively avoided further education institutions, thereby reducing the prospects of gaining skills and qualifications that are valued in the labour market). The same study also indicated a tendency towards 'levelling-down' among some excluded com-munities, where individuals who 'got above themselves' were viewed with suspicion and mistrust; this was particularly the case for adults, and especially for women (Field, 2005, pp. 65–71).

Social capital and cultural capital can both reinforce one another in promoting educational achievement; in Bourdieu's terms, however, they also help to reproduce educational inequalities. However, Bourdieu was wrong to define social capital as something that almost exclusively functioned to preserve privilege. While it certainly can perform this function, Coleman's work is notable for demonstrating that low income and minority communities can create network resources that then help them use education in order to over-come other sources of disadvantage.

Innovation and knowledge transfer

Just as lifelong learning has risen up the policy agenda since the 1980s, so has the importance increased on innovation and knowledge transfer. Moreover, all of these have become increasingly significant for all types of organisations, including companies, as they seek to improve performance in response to external competitive pressures. They are indeed closely related to one another, a relationship sometimes expressed in the language and aspiration of the knowledge economy or learning economy. These ideas have particular appeal in the high-wage economies, where old competitive advantages such as location near sources of skilled labour, raw materials or product markets are losing their importance. In a globalised world economy, where technology and science are virtually ubiquitous, competitive advantage stems increasingly from the capacity to innovate and adapt. Of course, this is not an absolute: the success of low-fare airlines is merely one example of the continuing advantages of strong cost controls, even if this means reducing spending on training and customer service. Nevertheless, sustainable high-wage economies can only prosper through constant innovation and knowledge transfer.

Increasingly, economists acknowledge that there is a marked social dimension to economic growth. Much knowledge transfer takes place because of investments in human capital: specialist workers are able to copy ideas and techniques from elsewhere and apply the same scientific discoveries to different processes. In principle, knowledge transfer is usually presented as a very straightforward, one-way process. However, the innovation process is not a simple one. First, people may reasonably decide that they do not wish to share new ideas and methods with their competitors; a whole industry of copyright and patent protection is growing up around precisely this concern. Second, much knowledge is context-specific; especially in service industries, where suppliers interact directly with customers, it is important to understand and take account of local laws, languages and cultures. Third, the value of much knowledge depends on the ways in which it is applied. While general principles may be codified and transmitted relatively easily, it is not always possible to specify precisely just how a particular tool or technique works in a particular environment. Much knowledge – including many practical applications – is tacit, or embedded in specific social networks with their largely unquestioned routines; indeed, these networks are often creating and re-creating knowledge, rather than simply engaging in a series of one-way knowledge transfers.

For economists then, the rapid diffusion of knowledge can present something of a problem. While it is relatively easy to transfer standardised and codified knowledge from one setting to another, it is precisely this form of knowledge that is most easily protected in legislation. This places all potential users on much the same footing: provided they are willing either to pay the owner of the intellectual property or take the risk of legal action, they are all able to adopt the same methods and innovate in the same ways. While this may certainly lead to productivity gains across the board, it does little to secure a sustainable advantage. In this case, the advantage goes to those whose costs are lowest – and usually this will be because they are operating in a low-cost labour market.

Hence the significance of social capital, and particularly of networks, reciprocity and trust. As a number of economists now acknowledge, tacit and embedded knowledge are most easily promoted where high levels of trust exist between established networks of workers and firms (Cooke, 2002; Lundvall and Johnson, 1994; Kim and Nelson, 2000). Survey data has been analysed to show that social capital is at least as strongly associated with economic growth as more conventional assets such as human capital (Whiteley, 2000). As with participation in learning, macro-level findings need to be treated with caution, not least because researchers are generally forced to rely on proxy indicators for social capital; while far from useless, these indicators are certainly not a direct fit. Nevertheless, the survey data do suggest that there is some association between connectedness and growth.

A number of studies at regional and company level have also drawn attention to networks as a channel for innovation and competitive advantage (Porter, 2000). Firms that lack access to more conventional business assets, such as financial and human capital (or well-endowed research departments), are particularly likely to depend on interpersonal networks. In the UK, for example, small firms are much more likely to cooperate with scientists if they are located near a university; while proximity may help promote cooperation with larger companies, by contrast, it is not an essential pre-requisite (Lambert, 2003, p. 79). Maskell's study of the Danish furniture industry shows that, despite high labour costs, the industry remains internationally competitive because of close ties between workers and managers in different firms, leading to willingness to share ideas and information (Maskell, 2000). Even well-established firms with good access to more conventional resources benefit from reductions in transaction costs arising from trust-based relationships.

So far, so good: social capital appears to promote innovation and knowledge transfer, to the benefit of all concerned. People are willing to share with competitors because they expect to benefit themselves, if not now then at some later stage, and because they trust the competitor to play fair with them. As in the case of lifelong learning though, there can also be a number of negative dimensions. The first is that, just as networks can reinforce innovation and dynamism, so they can reinforce conservatism and 'lock-in', so that entrepreneurs find new ways of getting more out of old methods and techniques rather than investing in change (Field, 2005, pp. 72–3). Second, the problem of 'insiderism' is a potential feature of network-based economic development. Those who are in a network may have a vested interest in keeping others out, in order to limit the competition. These divisions can easily run along ethnic lines, and thus help to reproduce existing inequalities. Third, people can engage in rent-seeking behaviour through networks; for example, individuals can focus on doing one another favours, rather than pursuing collective goals. Fourth, innovative business clusters tend to develop in regions which are already endowed with key resources, such as universities or natural assets (Rosenfeld, 2002, p. 19). And finally, business networks can have a 'dark side': they can share information on how to cut corners, evade legislation on such issues as food hygiene, occupational health or pollution control, and help members work out how to avoid paying tax (Field, 2003a, pp. 71–90). Few discussions of clusters and business networks pay attention to these negative aspects; nor does the conventional literature normally attend to issues of equity and justice.

Once again, then, we see a complex relationship between social capital and economic behaviour. While there is general evidence to support the proposition that social capital promotes innovation and sustainable growth, the pattern is not clear-cut. It seems that networks and trust-based relationships are important in many business contexts, but there is relatively little evidence either way on the impact of civic engagement and associational membership. There are also signs that people can use their networks to pursue unscrupulous goals, which may cut across efforts at innovation and sustainability, as well as undermining the legitimacy of business growth policies.

Policy ambivalence and possible solutions

In these circumstances, policy makers and educators might be forgiven for throwing up their hands in horror. Academics are notorious for demonstrating conclusively that the world is a complex place and the debate on social capital is certainly no exception. While it is widely accepted that people's networks can play an important role in helping them realise their goals, the complexities mean that the law of unintended consequences penalises all but the most sensitive policy interventions. Examples are not hard to come by: later in life, James Coleman bitterly regretted the policy reception of his own report on equality of educational opportunity, since measures such as bussing had helped to damage the very communities that he had examined in his research, and probably contributed more to diminishing rather than increasing the educational opportunities of African-Americans (Coleman, 1990, pp. 69–74). While the idea of social capital can be a helpful one for asking new questions about policy, whether in education or business growth, it certainly does not offer policy makers a magic bullet.

The promotion of networks and linkages as a focus for policy does not necessarily lead to direct, or even indirect, benefits to low-income groups, small firms and disadvantaged regions. The first requirement for policy is then, that public support for networks and clusters should be based on a clear expectation of social benefits. This means turning the conventional critique on its head: rather than lamenting the equity risks associated with networks and clusters, policy should frame equity programmes around clusters (Rosenfeld, 2002, p. 16). This means tackling a whole range of systematic obstacles to full participation in clusters and networks.

Priorities will of course vary depending on local contexts. Nevertheless, it is relatively easy to identify the main factors preventing people from accessing the benefits that arise from networks and clusters, as well as reducing their chances of making an effective contribution to them (Rosenfeld, 2002). Unsurprisingly, the first is skills and knowledge (including affective as well as cognitive capabilities). These are needed in order to engage fully in network-based approaches to community and economic development, and also in order to take advantage of the opportunities that are subsequently created. In turn, this implies that education providers are able to engage with network-based approaches, and feel able to develop local demand-led programmes.

Second is the importance of 'bridging ties' that span different communities. Traditional community development strategies were designed to build solidarity within low income or excluded communities; many business cluster strategies are intended to strengthen bonds within a particular grouping of firms. By consolidating such 'bonding ties', these approaches then reinforce external boundaries, and increase reliance on internally available resources. This parochialism in turn creates exclusionary pressures, which cut off access to resources that are only available outside the grouping. In particular, it forms a barrier to dissonant information and ideas, which may challenge the accepted wisdom of the grouping. Yet it is precisely such dissonant material which provokes the richest learning, particularly when it undermines previously unquestioned articles of faith.

This points to the third important factor, the role of intermediary actors. In building bridging partnerships, policy makers often identify intermediary bodies who enjoy the trust of at least one of the core sets of stakeholders. Yet the majority of these bodies tend to be run and staffed by people who come from a social service or community organising background, rather than from business or the professions. This means that they 'have much stronger ties to the supply side, i.e. the individuals that need help of educational institutions, than to the demand side' (Rosenfeld, 2002, p. 40). Little wonder that exclusionary tendencies seem almost insuperable. Exceptions include some of the personal advisers appointed under the New Deals for benefit claimants in the UK; a study of the New Deal for Musicians points to the impact of personal advisers with an industry background, who are able to 'talk the talk' on both ends of the bridge, and can therefore explain each side to the other (Cloonan, 2004).

Finally, we can no longer take 'social literacy' for granted. In a complex globalised network society, in which individuals are becoming increasingly reflexive and mobile in their social relations, we cannot assume that traditional socialisation processes – family and school – will provide young people with the social capabilities and affective understandings that they need. As Barbara Misztal has noted, the very relaxed and open nature of contemporary social relationships produces a 'tyranny of informality' in which 'the forced imposition of an artificial equality' may undermine private/public boundaries, inhibit communication and produce a constant examination of the self (Misztal, 2000, p. 239). At the same time, our every-day life is increasingly pluralistic, involving us in transactions with people coming from a variety of lifestyles and cultures, some new and baffling, others equally unfamiliar but appealing to what are presented as ageless traditions and religions. In these circumstances, people find that their well-being and even safety depends on their ability to read and make sense of a bewildering variety of symbols and signs that others present in everyday encounters. I would therefore argue strongly for investment in social literacy, not only for young people but also for adults, including older adults for whom much of the new social etiquette feels like both mystery *and* threat.

How can such elements and strategies be developed and pursued? Which organisations are in a position to assume a leadership role? Do they have legitimacy among all the key actors? These are particularly acute questions in the UK, where local government has been stripped of its powers in recent decades, and no real layer of regional government exists (other than the so-called 'devolved governments' of Wales, Scotland, and – when it is not sus-pended – Northern Ireland). What are the alternatives to elected authorities, and do they carry the same (or even more) legitimacy to them? Are elected bodies equally legitimate to all members of the community, or have they failed to command the respect of precisely those with whom this chapter is concerned – low income populations, small firms and disadvantaged regions? But are newly-created government-sponsored coalitions really the answer, and if so how can they be maintained for sufficient time to build trust-based relationships with their key constituencies? Either we need to renew and reinvent local government, or we need to find alternative coalitions of governance that have sufficient longevity and legitimacy to command respect and trust, and that can allocate resources to network-based strategies that also attend to issues of equity and justice.

In summary then, social capital is an independent variable that explains at least some variations in capabilities for productive learning, by both individuals and by organisations. Ignoring it in policy and practice is to overlook something that stares us in the face. But the policy implications are challenging and complex. People whose social capital consists mainly of close ties, and where their bonding connections are with others who have low levels of human capital, are very likely to enjoy very limited access to ways of acquiring and generating new skills and knowledge; their network resources are usually only good at providing them with coping skills. Access to a variety of heterogeneous ties, by contrast, offers a highly effective way of accessing and generating a broad range of new knowledge and skills. Yet at the same time, heterogeneous networks may well promote types of learning that are challenging and even disruptive of existing social arrangements; precisely because they provoke innovative and creative responses, variety in networks can also cause people to ask why they maintain their involvement in particular relationships, and encourage them to explore alternatives. So all in all, the impact of social capital on learning is complex and is always bound up with other factors. What looks initially like an appealingly simple slogan – 'Invest in social capital' – turns out to be a rather more difficult set of judgements and choices. Seen from an equity perspective though, these challenges represent choices to be made and problems to be tackled. They are certainly no reason for standing back and wringing our hands in dismay.

Chapter 6

On a lighter note: social capital and educational policy: an imaginary conversation

Tom Healy

Senior Statistician, Department of Education and Science, Republic of Ireland[1]

Introduction

This chapter offers an imaginary conversation involving a Minister for Education and a senior policy adviser. It is about the meaning and relevance of the term 'social capital' to public policy and practice. It focuses particularly, by way of illustration, on the management of learning and schooling. The Minister, the Right Honourable Jeremy Earthly, is puzzled, curious, politically shrewd and sceptical. The adviser, Sir Olly Smoothly, is zealous, insightful and astute, if not somewhat naive. In the course of the exchange one might surmise that Smoothly is quite possibly morally and intellectually right in his argument. But is he politically correct and administratively practical?

Telling the parable touches on important issues. The crucial and relevant nature of these issues should not be missed in the course of this constructed humorous exchange. The conversation – which could have been adapted from the popular 1980s British TV series, *Yes Minister* – may not be so far-fetched and unreal as one might initially assume.

'Social capital' is a challenging concept. It can lead us to ask particular kinds of questions. It can also be upsetting, annoying and disturbing, if not downright confusing. It may also be dangerous. Martin Mowbray (2004a) has pointed to ways in which the notion of social capital can be used for political purposes. In the Australian examples he quotes, it would appear that the term is a convenient one for arguing that the State should do less and leave issues of social equity and cohesion to the many small platoons of volunteers. This charge has echoes as far away as Ireland.

In the second part of the original Hot Topic paper a more serious style emerges (Healy, 2005). What can we do *now* – as policy-makers, politicians, civil servants, teachers, community workers or just ordinary folk? That paper touches on the complex and fraught issue raised by Martin Mowbray – could social capital become a distraction in a world of injustice and inequality where the real question is about who owns, controls and allocates economic, social and political resources?

Yes minister, no minister, maybe

A conversation between two education policy makers somewhere.

Venue: Minister's Office, Ministry of Education and Cutting-Edge Research (MECER), Ordinaryland.

Minister: Rt. Hon. Jeremy Earthly

Senior Policy Adviser: Sir Olly Smoothly

Biographical details:
Rt. Hon. Earthly: Member of Parliament from the rural constituency of Middle-Earth in the far south and recently appointed Minister of Education having served as Minister for the Post Office.

Sir Olly: Chair of the Institute of Advanced Interdisciplinary Studies at the University of Atlantic Philatelist Foundation, Senior Policy Adviser on secondment to MECER, former Director of the Division for School Reconstruction at the International Bank for the Reduction of Conflict.

Minister (M): Look, Smoothly, I wanted to talk to you about something that has been coming up at recent cabinet discussions. You know that the Prime Minister is keen on this business of 'social capital'. Can you remind me again what all of this means? And I don't have much time as I have to chair the cabinet sub-committee on Value-For-Money in Public Executive Agencies beginning within an hour's time.

Smoothly (S): Certainty, Minister. Social capital is very simple. It is about how people relate to each other – in neighbourhoods, organisations, families – even schools.

M: Even MECER!?

S: Yes, Minister. You see, the number of contacts people have with each other, the extent to which they are involved in their communities and how they trust others, including those who are not like them…helps them to *get things done better.*

M: Yes, yes. But what has this to do with education; with schools?

S: Quite a lot, I think. Schools work better and students learn more if the places and communities in which they learn are well connected, supportive and 'joined-up'.

M: Well, that is pretty obvious anyway.

S: Yes, and there is a lot of research literature about the impact of 'social capital' on schooling and learning as well as the way in which schools and colleges contribute to 'social capital'.

M: Oh, not 'research evidence' again. I am tired of listening to Blueskies (Minister for Health – Ed.) at Cabinet. She never stops talking about the dramatic evidence for the impact of what she calls 'social networks and norms' on health, social equality and community well-being.

And then she goes on about bonding and bridging until I am black and blue from glue and super WD-40. Her initiative to ban smoking in pubs has pushed 200,000 adults into the freezing cold where more social capital has been created in the space of six months than 10 years – and it all cancels out the negative impact of smoking – so she says.

As she waxes on about all sorts of longish studies ('longitudinal' – Ed.) showing that depression and suicide are related to the number of associations people are members of and how many close friends they can trust, everyone else feels almost depressed.

And then she goes on and on about *autopoiesis* and self-organised living networks and that it is all to do with the *Gaia* as a leading universal principle and para-dime (paradigm? – Ed.). She used to be a senior lecturer in the Sociology of Animal Life. Enough said. Still, we must be careful – she almost resigned from the cabinet last year and pulled us into an election – before the hospital ward rationalisation scheme was reversed.

S: Does anyone respond to her?

M: Well, it gets rough treatment from Home Affairs. He says that what we need is more police on the beat and longer sentences, not a lot of wind about 'community norms' and 'empowerment'.

But, more seriously, the PM is interested. In fact, he lent me a copy of his *Bowling Alone* written by some American Academic – Putnam – remember all the interviews and press photos with the PM last year? Some columnist claimed that the PM had joined the Mennonites! [Shared chuckle] Actually, I must read this *Bowling Alone*.

S: You should – it is very easy to read, authoritative, clear and persuasive.

M: But, between you and me, the PM gives me two books to read each year – at Christmas and summer holidays. He says that he is going to give me *The Creative Class* by some other American guru soon, and I have not even finished *Bowling Alone*. I never seem to finish any book I begin since I entered Parliament 15 years ago. You met this Putnam, didn't you?

S: Yes, at a World Bank conference on social capital in 1999 where, after three days of gruelling econometrics, hordes of really nice social analysts showed that 'social capital' was really a tough concept able to perform as well as 'human capital' in explaining a lot of things – if only we had decent and better empirical measures?

M: What?

S: Well, anyway, none of the top-notch economists at the conference were having any of this 'social capital' nonsense. But, then arrived Putnam from tea with the Clintons at the White House and everyone was on-side.

M: Don't you think that all of this is risky given public opinion about the PM's handling of our relationships with the US?

S: It is nothing to do with politics – or with America. In fact, one of the main writers on social capital was Bourdieu – he was French and a bit lefty at that.

M: Oh yes, I remember Blueskies going on about that Boudon fellow or whatever you call him.

S: In practical terms, Pierre Bourdieu's take on social capital is a bit different to that of James Coleman and Robert Putnam – or so a lot of people are saying these days. For example, it is claimed that Bourdieu used the term to describe the way in which different families, social groups and power elites can use their social connections to advance their own interests.

Social capital is not always about cooperation: it can be about positioning yourselves in a particular group, political party or powerful or powerless network.

But then, Coleman goes on about power and exchange of interests in social networks and some people are now talking about linking social capital in addition to bonding and bridging. And furthermore…

[interruption] M: I'm lost – can we get back to schools?

S: Yes, Minister.

M: And standards?

S: Yes, Minister.

M: And accountability?

S: Of course, Minister.

M: What has all this 'social capital' talk to do with schools, curriculum and Value-For-Money. Does the 'capital' bit give me a handle on Value-For-Money? Actually, maybe it could make a good sound bite for my meeting this morning?

S: OK, Minister. Let's get straight to the point. You know that there is a proposal to close all two-teacher schools on cost-efficiency grounds.

M: I am being roasted daily by constituents down south.

S: And do you remember the furore over Post Office closures and the proposed introduction of delivery boxes at fixed points away from people's houses in the country?

M: Oh yes, we had to reverse the delivery box idea and soften the closure plan. We took a lot of stick from RAG (the Rural Ageing Group – Ed.) over that – they claimed that many older people would have nobody to talk to or look out for if the postal workers stopped at the front gate.

S: Or, anyone to look out for them.

M: Anyway, I suppose that Value-For-Money is good as long as it doesn't create too much political devaluation at the polls!

S: Exactly. And what is more, 'social capital' talk provides another way of looking at things. Take school size and school closure. If we can keep some small schools open, keeping children in their local neighbourhoods, then we might be able to encourage them to get more involved in their local community. And it would be easier for teachers, parents, students and many others to know each other and, I guess, 'check each other out'.

M: But, as my honourable colleague, Sir Meen Countit [the Minister of the Treasury with special responsibility for the National Office of Statistics – Ed.] keeps saying, 'If you can't count it, don't bother with it'.

S: Yes, Minister. But, then, not everything that can be counted counts.

M: Einstein said that, didn't he?

S: If we had some way of assessing the presence of 'social capital' in schools and local communities, we could enhance our SPAS [School Performance Audit System – Ed.]. Then, we might be able to measure the social value of investing in smaller schools, teams within schools, schools within collegiate networks of schools and criss-crossing partnerships of civil society and public institutions.

M: Blah, blah. Talking of SPAS – how are my schools doing down in Middle-Earth?

S: All of the secondary schools in your constituency were at least one standard deviation above the national target level on the new NLIUC

[Numero-Literacy-Information-Utilisation Capacity – Ed.] dumbed-down scale once everything else including ethnicity, gender, orientation, income and individuality were controlled for. Intriguing isn't it?

M: It's all due to the quality of our teachers down there, the benefits of the new Standardised National Curriculum I introduced last year, the in-service training programme and the longer-hours intervention programme for early children who were tested and found to be disadvantaged.

S: … and social capital?

M: How do you know?

S: I don't. But, I wonder if the fact that the inter-school variance on NLIUC scores has a high unexplained residual even controlling for ethnicity, gender, income and individuality should lead us to look beyond the school and individual student to other things that are happening in the community – and may I suggest in the specific types of communities you are only too familiar with, Minister, in Middle-Earth?

M: Don't give me the 'research says that further research is needed' line yet again – I am sick to the teeth of hearing that since I became Minister. Tell me what I should do. And by the way, I only have 40 minutes left before my VFM meeting.

S: With respect, Minister, I don't think that I can tell you what to do, nor do I think that you ought to tell schools, teachers, parents, students and others what to do. We need to hear what they are doing and *how* they do it.

M: But I am Minister at MECER. Surely I am elected and paid to find solutions to problems. We have policies and we have programmes. These must be improved. We must manage our public affairs better. Teachers must get back to teaching the core skills for a knowledge society.

And students must feel the pressure to learn and we need to know how well they are learning and how well they are taught by devising more comprehensive, more standardised, more efficient tests of all the core skills and competencies so that we can have world-class schools producing world-class graduates to compete in a globally competitive economy with widening access for all social groups to lifelong learning.

And this is what every sensible review group, OECD Study, World Bank Report, US Government and European Union communiqué has been saying for the last 20 years.

S: Yes, you are reading well from your drafted speech for next weekend's Secondary Heads conference. We will talk about that later this afternoon … but let's talk now about learning as something more than what is just taught in schools … something that involves networks of people conversing, meeting, trying out, linking.

M: Stop, you are beginning to go on like Blueskies. Enough.

S: Apologies, Minister. I was just trying to come back to the point that schools perform better when people talk to each other (I mean people like teachers for example), when parents are more involved with their kids and the school, when teachers trust the pupils in their classes and the pupils trust their teachers, when teenagers have someone to turn to at 3am in the morning when they don't see any point in going further, when learning is about trying out ideas and things together, when learning has some point – a goal, a passion, a vision, a spark that can get learners to feel that they are the ones writing their own curriculum.

Yes, but of course, we do need curriculum, national tests and SPAS tabling – but there has to be more to school and to schooling? What kinds of learning are we trying to encourage through schools for what kind of society?

M: You make a great speech-writer Smoothly, which is why I put up with you for now. But, give me six practical things I can do – new things or older things I can just do better. My term as Minister is as long as a piece of thread and we will have a general election within two years if Blueskies and her friends on the backbenches don't pull the rug in the meantime.

S: First, let go Minister. Let go Minister.

M: [in a loud and agitated voice] Never, never, I can't, I will not. People have to be accountable. We have to devise better systems to hold people to account and to control their actions. How can I trust anyone to be responsible when I can't always trust you, Smoothly?

S: By letting them be responsible. Trust yourself, Minister, to do it. Just do it.

JDI! Second, give people space and time to talk. It's called deliberative and sustained dialogue…Talk it Out. *TIO!*

M: Talking – that is all you academics ever do. I am not an intellectual. Nobody down in Middle-Earth uses words like 'social capital', 'sustained dialogue'. They expect me as Minister, and the government of which I am a part, to help them to find work, to improve their living standards, to keep their neighbourhoods safe, to improve hospital waiting times and to allocate more resource teachers to pupils with special needs.

S: OK, you don't have to use terms like 'social capital'. In fact it irritates a lot of my academic friends to hear people mixing 'social' and 'capital'. How about a combination of words that, shall we say, challenges … call it community … call it social cohesion … call it something that people understand or are prepared to hear? But, listen to their stories – how they do community and how they get things done without any MECER programmes. It is about communities developing and using their own resources – hidden, unique, gifted, shared – to solve their own problems.

M: But we know what their problems are. And, more importantly, we know what they lack. The *Study of Resource Needs and Deficiencies* which had been lying on my predecessor's desk before my arrival has outlined what *Target Groups* need, how they are deficient and lacking and what interventions are needed to resource them.

In fact, under the DAU [Deficiencies Audit Unit – Ed.] we have identified a set of 12 core deficiencies in NDAZ [Needy and Disadvantaged Area Zones – Ed.] with 50 SIs (Specific Interventions) to bring them up to the 25 SNAPs quantitative targets (Systematic Needs and Progress).

The 12,897 grant applications received from communities under the DAU have identified many weaknesses. In fact, communities are more aware of their deficiencies and need for retraining than ever before. This has been an outstanding contribution of my government to community development and this 'social capital' thing you are going on about. We are doing it: people like you are just talking about it.

S: But, only one of the 25 measurable SNAPs have been met so far, Minister – that one has already been met when the indicator was recalculated in a different way.

M: That is because we need a better and broader set of SNAP measures. We need a new data inventory.

S: Third, Minister, we need to encourage schools to get out into their communities and to help communities to get into their schools. We need to look again at the SPAS.

M: What do you mean?

S: Well, remember that Community Time Bank scheme launched in the Middle-Earth High School last spring.

M: Yes, I launched it.

S: It is linking hundreds of students with people in their neighbourhoods. People who hated schools are now turning up to language classes where fifth form students are coaching immigrants and the Small Business Association has given 3-month contracts to students to develop new local economy projects. I bet that their NLIUC scores will soar in the coming years.

M: We will see about that.

S: And what is more, the schools in Middle-Earth have started to open their doors at weekends and evenings to community groups. There is an air of excitement about the place and students are saying that they feel important, used, useful.

The teachers' unions have struck a deal with local school management boards to facilitate the Volunteer Programmes in the schools because teachers really feel part of the local community and have enjoyed sharing their expertise and experience with people they never knew or met before. Many parents have started to relax…

M: [loud and very agitated] Relax!!! What!!!! Never. This must be stopped at once.

S: … to relax about…well to relax about whether or not their kids will get 1,100 Matric points to enter the MacRip Elite Business Law school. What's more, the school trustees claim that schools are becoming bridging places and not just places of the same ethnic, religious and social background 'bonding'.

And to cap it all, the local branch of the teachers' union have given a surprise week away, in Tahiti, to the school head and her partner with a greeting: 'We just wanted to express our gratitude and love for all that you have empowered us to do'. Just imagine, Minister, our Permanent Secretary getting such a greeting from the National Executive of the same union!

M: Imagine my receiving such a message! But, words like 'love', 'trust', 'bonding', 'bridging' are *à la* Blueskies. Yuck! I am sick and I don't want the Minister of Health to heal me.

But what you are telling me, Smoothly, relates to a local thing – very good – but will it last? How can I mainstream this into a national programme that I can roll out within my remaining term? And how can we evaluate it and within what programme?

S: Minister, you don't have to roll out anything…just let people roll it out. Don't stand in the way. Encourage them.

M: You think that any of my other sensible advisers and officials would entertain this sort of vague, community soft-touch nonsense? We have budgets to manage, crises to deal with and organisations to run. And we have to survive from day to day.

S: And our survival is at stake because we are powerless – we are powerless because we have bought into a system of command and control where we have imagined and told everyone that we can plan, deliver, measure and succeed as ministers, policy-makers and administrators.

The truth is that our young people have never been more schooled – but are they well educated? Our teachers are demoralised because they feel like puppets. Our school heads are angry and frustrated because they have been turned into managers. Your colleagues, Minister, are fed up of listening to rhetoric about lifelong learning, widening access to education, the knowledge society…when schools and colleges don't really change and when they do, we are unsure if that is a good thing.

And the poor have moved up a notch to become even poorer relative to others who are moving up faster, and all our intervention programmes have not made much difference. And communities feel disempowered and young people feel more alienated from politics and civic life than when we were young. Have we invested our rhetoric and actions in a competitive world of human capital to the detriment of an inquiring, creative and co-operative world of social capital?

M: Here we go again with vague, moralistic verbosity. This is not the stuff of managing, staying popular and succeeding in a world where power, control and scientific measurement is the name of the game. Your game is not for me.

S: But, it is good for the country.

PAUSE

S: It could represent a fourth way – people are fed up and disillusioned. Everything else has been tried – first, second and third ways.

PAUSE

S: People would be inspired by your thoughtfulness, your courage – your *vision* for a new learning society that would release human potential as never before. They would say Earthly has something the others lack.

M: I can't stand you, Smoothly, but you are smart. Send me a memo. Maybe I will set up a cross-departmental group to look into the matter. I must be on my way now to the VFM meeting.

S: Shall I include the other three ideas I didn't have time to tell you about, Minister?

Minister has already left.

So what? [this section of extracts from Healy (2005) indicates the fuller scope of that paper – Editor]

Waiting for the results of more empirical research?
One approach is to conclude that it is much too early to draw firm conclusions about the implications of social capital research for public policy or community practice. On this basis, it is argued, we should develop new measures of social capital (volunteering, trust, engagement, network reciprocity) or make better use of existing ones.

Fortified with a much wider range of convincing evidence and empirical research it should be possible to (i) further demonstrate the importance of social capital for the wide range of outcomes of interest to policy makers and others; (ii) find out 'what works' in specific situations as a result of observing the impact of social capital over time – especially different observable types of social capital (bonding, bridging, linking, neighbourhood, familial, etc.); and (iii) observe and measure the impact of public policy and action on social capital (an important and often neglected area raised by Mowbray, 2004a).

Demonstrating the importance of social capital in (i), above, is now an established area of ongoing research. Finding out what works in (ii) might be part of a deliberate social experiment to try out various policy interventions and examine the impact of each on specific and observable outcomes. Depending on which experiments are consciously labelled 'social capital', (ii) is still relatively underdeveloped internationally. Track (iii) is where Martin Mowbray seems to see the maximum value for a new round of social capital research – how do government actions affect public trust, engagement and community connection? With (iii) the locus of attention is back to government; here Mowbray suggests that classic Putnam social capital analysis has been weak up to now.

All three tracks miss a crucial point because each stems from an essentially empiricist foundation. I argue that we need both to:
- continue clarifying, refining, observing, measuring (where possible and sensible) and researching social capital; and at the same time to
- interact with policy-makers and community practitioners about us as 'co-researchers' and 'co-practitioners' even if we can't measure every dimension of social capital.

[Doing and learning from research]
[The benefits of empirical research]

The limitations of empirical research
Returning to social capital, if we can liberate the notion from having to perform a ballet dance at the empiricist opera then we might make sense of how it challenges present-day policy and practice.

In the imaginary conversation, the Minister was looking for 'solutions' on the basis of hard evidence. It was so terribly obvious as to be incontrovertible. Why wouldn't he seek more evidence and data? And surely the business of government is to 'govern', especially if it has any conscience in relation to the needy and the discriminated in society. Earthly was right. But so was Smoothly. The problem was that they hadn't (a) fully listened to each other and (b) thought through seriously the implications of their conversation.

It is very doubtful whether a lot more data, indicators and complicated statistical analysis would have enabled either Earthly or Smoothly to discover *what* to do in relation to *specific* issues of programme design and delivery or *general* issues of expenditure, legislative or administrative priority-setting. More and better quality data might, at best, confirm what they had concluded from other sources of evidence including on-going conversations, observation and interactions with various other people. More data might tilt them in the direction of particular priorities.

The new public policy agenda
Effective policy skills might enable us to:
- cultivate mutual help and self help in others;
- identify the 'capabilities' in others – as well as their needs/ deficits;
- promote trust through equality and respect for rights;
- let go of excessive and over-detailed control (thus empowering and trusting individuals and communities to be more responsible); and
- value, reward and recognise voluntary effort and achievement.

In a policy-plurocratic world as distinct from a policy-bureaucratic one, the State at local or national level moves to being supportive and enabling more than controlling.

Some questions
1. Is social capital something that Governments need to consciously invest in? If so, which areas need attention and recognition?
2. Or, is it enough that Governments are aware of the importance of social capital in different spheres? Might being aware influence how they go about their business?
3. Is social capital best abandoned as a term – should we get back to talking about social inclusion/exclusion, social partnerships and community development? Why add a new term to an already crowded space – conceptually, politically and analytically?
4. Could 'social capital' provide 'value-added' to existing areas of policy focus: social inclusion, sustainable natural environment, regional economic innovation systems, care of the elderly, etc.?

5. Do we need a 'social capital' desk somewhere in Government (PM's office, Community Affairs, Local Government)?
6. Is social capital another nuisance – a new form to be filled in or a gratuitous system of terms to be incorporated into visionary-futurist speeches of the Minister?

[*What about accountability?*]

And, what about the equality agenda?

Social capital is too convenient for middle-of-the road politicians, it might be said. No wonder some senior politicians warm to 'communitarianism' – it represents cheap talk, costs nothing and appeals to a lot of people but delivers little by way of real change. This is a view I have heard expressed more than once. Martin Mowbray presented this view clearly and forcefully in his Hot Topic (Mowbray, 2004a).

New communitarianism – a necessary bête noire for egalitarians?

Not infrequently, social capital is perceived as competing with social equality. The association and confusion of social capital literature with claims about changes in family structure, public morality, the role of women and the benefits of voluntarism in social engagement raise suspicions. The suspicions are all the more easily raised when people ask 'who is sponsoring this notion and why?' If we took a little more time to listen to what is being said and the many different types of people saying it we might be less inclined to jump to conclusions that this is a socially conservative plot.

Mowbray (2004a) has a point: emphasising the role of civil society (and implicitly subsidiarity of public roles in favour of the State letting other parts of society take up a lead role) could indeed be a short-cut to public (State) disinvestments in social capital if we are looking at a social capital zero-sum game. Contracting out social capital to neighbourhoods, families, churches and voluntary bodies would indeed be a low-cost, privatisation of roles and responsibilities. But has it to be zero-sum game? Why couldn't the State be *more*, not less, proactive in building community capacity, at the same time letting go of top-down interference and inviting partnerships, synergies and co-responsibility?

What could a local or central public authority do to promote 'social capital'?

I have emphasised the facilitating role of State agencies in letting go and releasing valuable energies and potential. What more can public agencies –

especially at the local level – do to increase trust, encourage greater participation and engagement at the grass roots? How can policies, programmes and public agency practice help to encourage people to be more sociable, trusting, supportive and connected to the extent that these are generally perceived to be public goods and positive ones at that for individuals and whole societies?

Education, spatial planning and effective community-support measures provide just three examples of ways of strengthening social capital at local level – or rather letting social capital loose where it is under-utilised or effectively forbidden.

Lifelong learning is the key to social capital

It cannot be assumed that human and social capital are necessarily complementary in every case. For example, strong familial or ethnic ties might inhibit individuals or groups, women, for example, from pursuing further studies or social advancement through self-directed learning. On the other side, a narrow, individual focus on education may isolate individuals and groups from their immediate communities and reinforce a sense of exclusion or isolation.

The balance of evidence (reviewed in OECD, 2001b) suggests that communities rich in social capital, as measured by higher rates of community involvement and trust, tend to record higher rates of participation in education as well as higher school achievement, used as proxy measures of human capital. There are good theoretical and practical reasons for such complementarity. Knowing is essentially a relationship among subjects; knowing is social. We are innately both learning and social creatures by virtue of evolutionary development (Abbott and Ryan, 2000). Relationships of trust and reciprocal engagement presuppose particular skills and attributes of individuals. In the other direction, learning habits and effective learning and knowledge transfer presuppose a social setting in which people can learn in relationship with others.

Learning to cooperate, communicate and engage for a more open, tolerant and active civil society is important for the development of social capital and well-being. In the economically developed world, schooling is an important experience for a large part of almost every person's life. Even if, at most, 20 per cent of total 'waking time' is spent by young people (aged 6–15) in school, the impact of school on behaviour, attitudes and preparedness for work and life is profound. Being educated along with others as well as being involved in social activities is one of the most effective ways of getting to know (and respect) others of different social, ethnic, religious, political or cultural backgrounds.

Schooling is a natural area in which public authorities can exert long-term influence on social capital, in partnership with learners, families and communities. This can work at both local and national level. At a national level, a reformed approach to curriculum, pedagogy and assessment could provide a huge benefit in terms of improving social cohesion. The involvement of communities and learning partnerships of students, teachers and parents in governance, curriculum design and implementation at local and national level is important. So is the content and process of learning in schools in so far as these help foster positive civic attitudes and behaviour.

Experiential learning in a relevant social context
A key policy challenge is to embed learning in the workplace as well as social and community practice. Too often formal education has tended to isolate the learner from 'practice' and from 'other learners.' There is a need to reconnect schools, homes and communities in the widest sense. Peter Senge speaks not just of schools but schools that learn because they are comprised of learning communities themselves (Senge et al., 2000).

[*A case in point: institutional reform in higher education*]

Concluding remarks

Public policy needs to facilitate dialogue, exchange and sharing of some public norms. The way in which information flows, the patterns of engagement and empowerment, and the content and quality of social interaction matter as much as the mere existence of social connectedness. Much of the policy challenge in relation to social capital is to identify ways of recognising and empowering it. Public institutions like schools, local authorities, civic fora and community councils can provide crucial 'nodes' in which these social connections and conversations can take place across existing social, ethnic and cultural boundaries. If our sole starting point for public policy is conflict over resources and addressing inequality then we risk staying stuck in a narrow model of control. If we ignore issues of social inequality, power relationships and context in a generalised attempt to promote social capital we can also get stuck in another narrow model of control – one in which social and cultural differences are left out of the equation.

The best way to promote social capital is through policies and practices that favour inclusion, trust-building initiatives to recognise, respect and empower both communities and genuine equality of opportunity. The best way to promote equality is through enhancing community spirit and participation in a way that builds social consensus around an equality agenda. If, for example, we wish to increase taxes to pay for more social services at local level, people may be more inclined to support higher local taxes if they see where their money is going, and if they feel they have more direct control over its use at municipal or county level.

Those on the political left should see in the idea of social capital an opportunity to empower civil society in partnership with the State. In this way social capital becomes for them a complement rather than a threat, as seemed to be the case in the initial reactions to the notion of social capital in political discourse in Ireland. Those on the political right (if such terms retain validity or utility any longer) need to accept social capital as a way of counter-balancing the excesses of markets that under-produce effective social norms and institutions. Those in academia need to accept that social capital has little meaning or validity unless the normative, practical and heuristic value of the concept is acknowledged and explicitly linked to social action.

Epilogue

Minister Earthly had a point. Smoothly hadn't known that the Minister's favourite book of *realpolitik* was not *Bowling Alone* but Maciavelli's *The Prince*. In it, it is written:

> And it ought to be remembered that there is nothing more difficult to take in hand, more perilous to conduct, or more uncertain in its success, than to take the lead in the introduction of a new order of things. Because the innovator has for enemies all those who have done well under the old conditions, and lukewarm defenders in those who may do well under the new. This coolness arises partly from fear of the opponents, who have the laws on their side, and partly from the incredulity of men, who do not readily believe in new things until they have had a long experience of them. Thus it happens that whenever those who are hostile have the opportunity to attack they do it like partisans, whilst the others defend lukewarmly, in such wise that

the prince is endangered along with them. (from Chapter VI of *The Prince* by Nicolo Machiavelli)

Earthly has just given Smoothly a brand new copy. Having made a call to Highgate Cemetery in London where Karl Marx was buried, Smoothly has already scrawled on the back on the inside title page:

Up to now philosophers (social scientists) have sought to interpret the world (to explain, measure, define diverse social phenomena): *the point is to change it.*

Workers of the world (policy makers, practitioners, researchers, ordinary folk) *unite!*: you have nothing to lose but your chains (disciplinary ones where we end up thinking the same thing and assuming that the world is rectangular because the only people we talk to, meet and work with believe more or less the same thing).

Notes

[1] Any views expressed in this chapter are those of the author and do not reflect those of the Department of Education and Science in Ireland.

Chapter 7

Tales of resilience from two Finnish cities: self-renewal capacity at the heart of strategic adaptation

Markku Sotarauta

Introduction

Human history is full of successes and failures; time and again we have witnessed how life alternates between joy and sorrow. Occasionally we live stable and peaceful times, but quite often our lives are shaken by major economic and societal transformations. During the last decade or two we have once again seen, in a very concrete manner, how the world is changing. Some cities have risen in prosperity; others have declined. New professions have come into being; old ones have receded into history. The future seems to be an open, constantly evolving entity. It is not something waiting somewhere around the corner only to be anticipated and planned for. The future is being discovered, created and shaped all the time; it is emerging from manifold processes.

The early twenty-first century seems to be dominated by an almost compulsive need to find new pathways to the future. All over the world policy-makers have been chasing new buzzwords for their endeavours to show how dynamic their city-regions are. In ten years we have witnessed a rapid flow of key ideas, concepts ranging from clusters to networks, from knowledge to innovation and from learning to creativity. Many city-regions have indeed changed according to these lines and many policy-makers have found new food for thought. So, the new practices of economic development policy in the city-regions range from pure rhetorical gimmicks to dynamic action. Sometimes it is difficult to distinguish these two extremes from each other.

It is always easier to uncover the elements of success and/or failure in retrospect than to find new development paths for the future and new modes of action in the middle of uncertain and open-ended situations. Quite often development surprises policy-makers, sometimes the surprise is pleasant and sometimes less so. Even the most 'learned of the city-regions' with well-developed foresight capacity encounter unexpected situations every now and then. At all events, city-regions need to continually find out how to adapt to a changing environment without ending up as captives to their economic fate; and it seems that resilient regions cope with the changes better than less resilient ones (Sotarauta and Srinivas, forthcoming). In resilience, strategic adaptation emerges as crucial. In strategic adaptation, both adaptation to the changing environment and the strategic choices of actors play a significant role. Strategic adaptation, in general, endows regions with a capacity to change their destiny by adapting themselves to changes and reshaping their local selection environments.

This chapter examines the answer to the question how localised adaptation processes, institutions and intentions of a policy network drive strategic renewal, and hence the discussion centres on what the key elements of self-renewal capacity of city-regions are. The approach adapted here emphasises both policy intentionality and emergent developments, and in this kind of setting self-renewal capacity emerges as a key concept. For me self-renewal capacity represents, on the one hand, a way to understand how policy intentionality and emergence encounter each other in the practices of economic development. On the other hand, self-renewal capacity directs our attention to those functions and processes that ought to be embedded in the economic development of city-regions one way or another. To highlight the significance and the main functions and processes of self-renewal capacity I draw especially on empirical observations from the Local Innovation Systems' project[1].

From creativity, innovation and learning to self-renewal capacity

Transformations

In the early 2000s, city-regions are engaged in a fiercer global rivalry than ever before in creating or attracting wealth-generating activities for their citizens. There now exists a large body of studies stressing that both localised and global sources of knowledge are crucial in competitiveness of city-regions. These knowledge pools may arise from the concentration of sectorally or cluster-specific firms and other relevant organisations. Bathelt et al. (2004) suggest that both 'the information and communication ecology created by co-location of people and firms within the same industry and place or region and global pipelines, i.e. channels used in accessing knowledge external to city-region, offer advantages for organisations engaged in innovation and knowledge creation'. As they state:

> local buzz is beneficial to innovation processes because it generates opportunities for a variety of spontaneous and unanticipated situations, global pipelines are instead associated with the integration of multiple selection environments that open different potentialities and feed local interpretation and usage of knowledge hitherto residing elsewhere. (Bathelt et al., 2004)

In an industrial society, borders between nations, institutions, organisations, municipalities, and so on largely determined the position of city-regions; in a global economy, however, borders are fuzzier than before. Now the positions of both organisations and regions are determined by their competencies and skills to learn and develop themselves in a continuous process (Sotarauta and Bruun, 2002), this seems to be leading to a polarised development through increased differentiation in innovation and economic growth between the 'successful' and the 'unsuccessful' regions (Asheim and Dunford, 1997). It also seems that fortunes change and that the 'successful' ones may lose their touch in the global economy; fortunes have certainly changed during the transformation from an industrial to knowledge-based economy.

As Safford (2004) states, the Silicon Valleys of the Second Industrial Revolution had names like Akron, Detroit, Pittsburgh, and Rochester; in Europe we might add Ruhr and Manchester; and from the Finnish point of view, Tampere, the birthplace of industrial Finland, should be added to the list of 'industrial stars'. The stars of the industrial era have been forced to find a new position in a new situation. For example, in Tampere, three major trans-formation processes have taken place. First, the textile industry declined and disappeared (only a few highly specialised textile firms have survived). Second, against a background of industrial recession dating back to the oil crisis of the 1970s and severe national economic recession of the early 1990s, the engineering industry succeeded in reinventing itself through renewing and developing technology of an increasingly high level. Third, new and rapidly growing business sectors emerged; particularly in the 1990s, the information and telecommunications technology clusters grew rapidly (see Sotarauta and Srinivas, 2005; Martinez-Vela and Viljamaa, 2004; Kostiainen and Sotarauta, 2003).

Another Finnish city, Turku, did not face such industrial transformation as Tampere, and hence it did not have such external triggers to force it to move into new policy-making regimes, as was the situation in other case-regions mentioned here. It was not until the 1990s that Turku faced the need to redefine itself. At that time, national recession and fiercer global competition resulted in a slow decline in its economic base, and therefore attention of policy-makers turned to the emerging biotechnology cluster (Srinivas and Viljamaa, 2003).

Policy directions

Even though the transformation processes have their local characteristics, at a general level the nature of transformation from industrial to knowledge economy has many similarities in different parts of the world. Globalisation also seems to lead towards a convergence of development strategies. A few years ago, learning regions were appearing in different parts of the globe, and now, in the early 2000s, policy-makers all over the world aim, at least in their main speeches and development documents, to attract a 'creative class' by enhancing tolerance and developing cultural offerings (Florida, 2002). Creativity has become very fashionable. It is global 'pop, must and in', and in addition, the modern evergreen of development policies – clusters – are alive and well. In addition, a huge literature on science, innovation, technology, expertise, and interaction-focused studies has emerged (see Camagni, 1991; Storper, 1995; Brazcyk et al., 1998; Florida, 1995; Maskell, 1996; Morgan, 1997; Kautonen et al., 2002; Cooke, 2002; Sotarauta and Bruun, 2002) and policy-makers in many regions have indeed sought to counter the decline in traditional industries and the challenge of a globalised economy by developing new knowledge-based high-technology clusters and enhancing interaction between academia and firms. It seems to be clear that all this is not just rhetoric; but both research and policy are greatly affected by these developments.

Economic transitions have led to new policy regimes. Tampere is one of the Finnish examples of how the combination of a strong knowledge infrastructure, corporate vision and leadership, and active local economic development policy can succeed in avoiding the fate of so many old industrial regions

(Martinez-Vela and Viljamaa, 2004). However, the building of new local capabilities began much earlier, in the 1960s, when Tampere was active in inducing two universities to move from Helsinki to the city. Tampere has indeed been, in many ways, influential in building and changing the institutional set-up for knowledge production and education; hence, for decades, it has been instrumental in creating an institutional foundation for future clusters and innovations. Without the institutional rearrangements of the 1960s and 1970s, the Finnish ICT boom of the 1990s would not have touched Tampere, but with a proper institutional set-up in place, the information and telecommunications technology cluster was able to grow rapidly in the city.

In its transformation process Turku is a bit different from Tampere. Turku did not have such an ICT-focused educational and research basis as some other Finnish cities. Therefore it did not have the local capabilities needed to enable an ICT boom, and consequently, when facing the danger of hollowing out of its economic base, it aimed for a new identity in a high-technology arena by merging various sub-fields of research and development (R&D) using bio-technology such as food, materials, and pharmaceuticals. These efforts differ from many other Finnish cases in that the public sector has not played a very active role in the early stages of development. The emergence of a biotech-nology cluster in Turku is based on a strong university research activity in the fields of natural and medical sciences and the old pharmaceutical and diagnostic industry. The mobilisation of local resources and the successful attempts to influence national science and technology (S&T) policy have mainly been a result of a network of individuals working in industry and in universities, rather than a general strategy of the universities or local govern-ment. Resource-scarcity and national science and technology policies pushed the universities forward to new kinds of cross-university, cross-departmental work that have been particularly innovative and open to interactions with industry. Thus, although Turku cannot be labelled as 'new' in terms of its emergence, its creation of a new identity has been intentional (Srinivas and Viljamaa, 2003).

The basic puzzle

In regional development policy-making the aim is often to understand and direct the processes that lead to changes over time in the mix of products and services that are produced within city-regions. Therefore, the focus has been on a) *innovation*, for example, the first applications of new inventions, and also on *innovation systems* and *innovation environments* (mechanisms supporting innovation processes); b) *learning*, for example, the various ways by which new processes, products, technologies, and so on are absorbed by individuals, organisations, and systems; and lately also, rather prescriptively, c) *creativity*, in other words the fountainheads of innovation.

The main problem that policy-makers are faced with is how to adapt purposefully to a changing environment. In Europe at least, in their efforts to promote economic development, policy-makers' attention is traditionally directed to development programmes, systems, funding schemes, best practices, and so on. They quite often focus on grand efforts that gain visibility. Recently, as certain cases have demonstrated, efforts have been targeted at bringing universities and firms together and in doing so open new paths for competence-building, with varying degrees of success.

Promotion of knowledge-based economic development requires better understanding of how city-regions generate development from within. Here flexibility of existing institutions, structures and mind-sets is crucial. As Boschma states, 'policy-making has not traditionally been keen on flexibility', but it may be essential in stimulating innovation and creating truly innovation-supporting local environments with strong global pipelines. The local environment needs to be transformed if the region is to benefit from newly emerging technologies. At the same time, as Boschma points out, we need to acknowledge, that 'organisations and institutions usually do not adapt spontaneously due to the many inertial' forces. Consequently, restructuring old organisations and institutions, creating new ones, and making new connections emerge as crucial (Boschma, 2005).

The city-regions discussed above have aimed to do exactly this, but more or less as a reaction to a crisis on hand; they have been forced to change, to adapt to a changing environment. However, quite often the reactionary policies are based on seeds planted years or decades earlier, often in the form of organisational institutions that have 'people working in the future' before the rest of us even realise that something is actually changing. For future crises we need to ask, more often than is currently the case, what kind of functions and processes are essential in an unbroken procession of reinterpretation and reinvention to enable entire city-regions to adapt strategically. In many city-regions that could be labelled resilient and that have been capable of bouncing back from industrial decline, concerted actions to adapt to the changing environment from within have played a crucial role in economic development, often in concert with various national policies.

Towards directed emergence

Many practitioners and regional development studies do not recognise confusion, ignorance and chance as forces causing and directing development. Policy often aims to eliminate uncertainty, but in thinking adopted here, various organisations engaged in economic development are seen to consist of 'people who do not always know what it is that they do not know, and therefore they do not know how they will react when they will know "it"' (Allen, 1990, p. 569). Hence in this way of thinking ambiguity may be a source of innovation and development (Sotarauta, 1996; Lester and Piore, 2004). This, as evolutionary approaches usually do, brings up the importance of uncertain and unexpected outcomes in the development of city-regions, and that reminds us that it is hard to predict where and when major transformations occur. Taking this kind of view seriously, we might end up concluding that policy-making does not have a role to play in directing the change processes. Dalum et al. (1992) state that this kind of evolutionary thinking implicitly favours non-intervention. So, there seems to be little room for effective policy-making, but as the cases suggest, policies have a role to play; in some cases they actually appear crucial. By no means is my intention here to propagate the idea of *laizzez-faire*, but instead to raise some notions on research and policy-making, drawing on evolutionary approach and emergence; hence the aim is, partly, to understand familiar policies from an alternative viewpoint.

Finding alternative entry points to economic development policies is important since new substance knowledge and information are emerging all the time which feed new insights to policy processes. But why are we not fully able to utilise new knowledge and insights; where are the lively visions and bold strategies when decisions are made? Why after good strategic planning procedures does everything seem to continue just as before? What prevents the visions from being created? I guess we know the answer all too well, drawing on Dryzeck (1993):

1) the general laws of society – on which it is believed the strategies of public actors can be based – are difficult to define in a watertight way, they are almost unattainable;

2) social goals are rarely pure and simple. Values are usually open to question, vacillating, and many-sided;

3) the intention of actors may override the causal generalisations of the policy-makers and planners. People may simply decide to do things differently;

4) interventions aimed at the course of development cannot be

empirically verified without the intervention being realised. (Dryzeck, 1993, p. 218)

I would add that in the economic development of city-regions we have a tendency to forget the diversity of human life and societies. Quite often strategic planning, for example, is about reducing uncertainty and ambiguity, but in resilient city-regions, I argue, ambiguity and emergence are not only problems but also, quite largely, sources of change and innovation.

The concept of emergence directs our attention to such qualities that appear 'from nowhere' as a result of many intertwined processes of numerous single organisations and individuals, and quite often it seems as if 'things simply happen' (Johnson, 2002). Emergence hence underlines the unpredictable nature of development and it is not goal-seeking or directed 'at the level of the whole' in the sense that there would be a specific desired outcome which could be planned and whose behaviour could be precisely predicted or controlled (Mitleton and Papaefthimiou, 2000). More specifically it can be defined as an overall system behaviour that comes out of the interaction of many participants and it cannot be predicted, even from the knowledge of what each component of a system does in isolation (Holland, 1998; McKelvey, 1999). Therefore, emergent systems as a whole develop organically and without any predestined goals, even though their elements, organisations and individuals have explicit goals to pursue. The capacity of emergent systems to learn, experiment, and grow is based on the general laws directing the elements (Johnson, 2002; Sotarauta and Srinivas, 2005).

Our earlier studies (Sotarauta and Srinivas, 2005) suggest that instead of linear policy-making we need directed emergence where the nexus of intentionality and freely-emerging processes is the crucial target of attention. Consequently, in policy-making we should be more sensitive in recognising the potential of emergent developments and the possible routes to the future, to finding the best possible policy-making approaches to each situation, location and time in question, in recognising the emerging processes, and not to create newly-invented policies from scratch. In practice, this suggests that policy-makers ought to know much more about what is going on in their own region to build on its existing strengths and capabilities to stimulate innovation. Policy-making could focus on directing local emergence, creating a local selection environment that buffers between local and global, responding to local problems, upgrading local institutions, strengthening connectivity between organisations, and so on (Boschma, 2005).

Based on the conceptual discussion and cases briefly discussed earlier in this chapter, the general conceptual framework in which self-renewal capacity of city-regions is rooted appears as in figure 7.1.

Figure 7.1 The basic conceptual frame for self-renewal capacity.

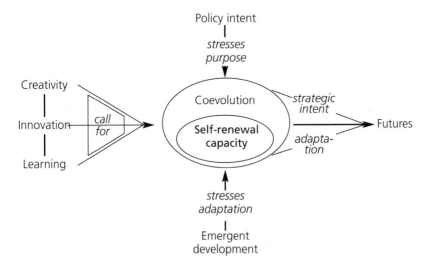

The main functions and processes of self-renewal capacity

Self-renewal capacity represents a set of processes that can be intentionally designed for the future on the one hand but are the core of adaptation on the other. Starting from the word *capacity*, and with a dictionary definition (Webster's), capacity can be defined to refer to a measure of the amount of work a system can perform, and also to the power of receiving and holding ideas, knowledge, etc. Hence if capacity refers to an ability to perform or produce something, self-renewal capacity can simply be defined as the set of capabilities targeted at renewing oneself in a continuous process; that is, the overall ability to deal with information, knowledge and innovation is crucial. In the context of economic development policies self-renewal capacity is by definition an attribute of several organisations and therefore one should always be aware of the question where in an ecosystem specific self-renewal functions are located, and how they are integrated into other functions. Tentatively, self-renewal capacity is based on the following functions: exploration, exploitation (problem-solving), absorption, integration and leadership.

Environmental selection theories emphasise that successful firms undertake similar strategic renewal activities and aim their actions at strengthening and exploiting existing core competencies. This is in contrast with theories stressing managerial intentionality that suggests that firms adapt by behaving differently and exploring new competencies (Flier et al., 2003). Most organisations display a tendency to prefer exploitation to exploration (March, 1991), and therefore there is a danger of falling into a 'competence trap' (Levinthal and March, 1993). Entire city-regions are also at risk of this, and it seems clear that, like individual firms, city-regions also need search processes at both a city-regional and cluster level. *Exploration* needs to be enabled so that emergent properties can be recognised as early as possible; hence strategic adaptation to changing situations is more likely than without exploration. As the cases suggest, those city-regions that have institutions, organisations and people engaged in explorative activities have a better chance of bouncing back than those city-regions whose explorative activities are fewer or non-existent.

Exploration can be deliberate, or it can be implicit and emergent. Exploration assets are integral to successful transition, but exploration is a difficult act for social entities, since the value of the existing asset profile is likely to be uncertain, and existing assets may bias the search and discovery process (Kash and Rycroft, 2002). Quite often, the economic development policy of a city-region provides various organisations with, more or less, an intentionally designed structure, but the question whether it adequately supports learning, exploration, and evolution emerges. Furthermore, do policies support divergence and variety, which are essential elements in triggering the emergence of new processes and products, and enabling the emergence of new modes of behaviour? City-regions can strengthen the institutional capacity for exploration, create and develop explorative spaces, increase variety, and make sure that there is enough attracting and rooting forces for the individuals engaged in exploration.

It may go without saying that exploration alone is not enough for continuous self-renewal, but the knowledge created in the explorative processes ought to be *absorbed*. Drawing on Cohen and Levinthal (1990, p. 569–570), '*absorptive* capability refers to abilities to identify, assimilate, and exploit knowledge from the environment'. Cohen and Levinthal have also argued that the ability to evaluate and use outside knowledge is largely a function of the level of prior related knowledge, and one might conclude that successful absorption is based on well functioning exploration. Absorptive capacity seems to be important for exploration too. Cohen and Levinthal (1990) suggest that the higher the absorptive capacity, the more likely it will be that the firm will focus more on opportunities provided by the environment, independent of current performance criteria. They even suggest that firms having well-developed absorptive capacity will tend to be more proactive; as they later state, 'fortune favours the prepared' (Cohen and Levinthal, 1994).

Outside sources of knowledge are critical to the self-renewal processes in general, and are also essential as parts of absorption, replication, and imitation of new knowledge, inventions, and innovations produced elsewhere. However, since direct replication without proper adjustment to local situations is seldom effective, interpretation is needed in fitting the new pieces and prevailing institutions and culture together. Interpretation in this context refers to collective sense-making processes where the respective system is either consciously or unconsciously reinventing its basic beliefs and assumptions of itself and the environment.

Quite often development and innovation processes operate in a *problem-solving* mode that is rational and clear-cut, often starting by identifying existing needs through to developing a new product or process that will best solve the problem. In this kind of process the task is broken into component parts and the resources are then organised to finalise the project. Strong problem-solving capacity may be crucial for entire industries to grow and to eventually end up renewing core competencies also (Martinez-Vela and Viljamaa, 2004). Not aiming to renew core competencies, problem-solving is quite largely based on exploitation, and even though short-term and pragmatic problem-solving produces more tangible and quicker solutions compared to exploration, city-regions ought to promote both exploration and exploitation processes with good capabilities in absorption and integration.

Integration refers to all those functions and processes that enable the combination of a versatile and many-sided set of information with actors and their competences and resources, for the adaptation, design and implementation of effective strategies and projects to promote regional competitiveness and hence to create a distinctive knowledge pool to form a core of competitiveness. Integration can be achieved through institutions, networking and socialisation (Sotarauta, 2005). Institutions refer to the webs of relations involved in development policies, which interlink public development agencies, firms, and educational and research institutes in more or less collective action, based on both strong and weak ties (Healey et al., 1999). Institutions frame the development efforts and processes, and provide activities at individual and organisational level. Of course, institutions may have either a positive or a negative influence.

Networking refers to the forging of mutual dependency, loyalty, solidarity and horizontal cooperation, based on trust and reciprocal support, among organisations and individuals. Socialisation refers to producing shared and often tacit knowledge that leads to the social integration of actors far beyond the institutions; networking, and the ability to network competently and efficiently to utilise informal relations, is significant. Therefore the ability to share feelings, emotions, experiences and mental models becomes important (Nonaka and Konno, 1998). In integration, as in absorption, interpretation is essential.

Leadership is also crucial for the self-renewal capacity of city-regions. Without proper leadership self-renewal capacity may remain static and turn out to be a hollow shell. Hence, leadership is the driving force in providing exploration, integration, absorption and problem-solving with direction, energy and vision and, most of all, in the context of economic development of a city-region, leadership is needed to cross the organisational, institutional and cultural boundaries and to aim for orchestrated efforts in a narrow isthmus between design and emergence. In this context, leadership is needed for directing emergence, not control. In general, leadership is required to build the organisation, institutions, structure and mental models for the future, that is, to secure new resources and develop new capabilities, and in doing so position the region and its organisations to take advantage of emerging opportunities and adapt to change (Sotarauta, forthcoming).

Conclusion

This chapter is largely concerned with change: how to cope with changes in the environment and how to stimulate change if the city-region is stagnating. Referring to the regional development or transformation of regions is easy enough so long as all one means by this rhetorical term is that regions change. The crucial issue is the mechanisms that produce this change; what sort of mechanisms play what sort of roles in the change in different contexts? The world of societal and economic change is full of hollow alterations and development rhetoric, and in contemporary discourse many kind of attributes are stressed for change. I see going back to basics as an important issue; hence we need to think more often than we are used to about how the capacity to change is embedded in the various systems.

Many scholars and practitioners alike stress teleological explanations – the importance of shared purpose, consensus and cooperation – as important factors in pursuing change. Others stress individual aims, competition, and scarce resources as crucial forces in economic change. I have stressed the need to better understand the co-evolution of emergence and policy intentionality, and, based on that, our capabilities to direct emergence. All in all, change is always a complex and not at all self-evident process. Rather, it may be depicted as adaptation to a changing environment in which organisations, universities, development agencies and individuals such as researchers and other experts have an active role to play, with many purposes that are in continuous interplay with the selection environment.

The basic message of this paper is that resilient city-regions are more likely to cope with rapid changes in the environment than those that are less resilient, and that the processes of self-renewal capacity serve in resilience. One of the main issues has been to tentatively identify what the key processes of self-renewal capacity are and to open the debate on how they may arbitrate between emergent development and policy intentions, how these processes interact, how the combination of individual processes affects the renewal of a city-region or a cluster, and how as a whole they shape the processes.

For policy-making, the basic message can be summarised as follows:
- In their economic policy-making, city-regions should stop attempting to directly imitate the latest global buzzwords and best practices, and instead adapt to the global economy by focusing more on actual local issues and capabilities.
- Development systems and policy-makers ought to serve the local emerging potential, people and organisations, and not vice versa as is too often the case.
- In policy-making it could be time to move from 'forcing partnership' to a 'real partnership' mode; therefore the arrogance of 'policy wisdom' should be scaled down and real open dialogue between relevant parties initiated.

Notes

[1] Coordinated by MIT/Industrial Performance Center other partners in the consortium being University of Cambridge/Centre for Business Research, Helsinki University of Technology/BIT Research Centre and University of Tampere/Sente (see http://ipc-lis.mit.edu/index.html).

Chapter 8

Kent: a virtual city-region

Donna McDonald*, Alison St.Clair Baker** and Robert Hardy**

*Kent County Council Corporate Services – Policy Unit, Kent, UK;
**Kent County Council Strategic Planning – Change and Development Division, Kent, UK

Introduction

This chapter tells the unfinished story of growth and regeneration in the county of Kent in south-east England and how Kent County Council is responding to the needs of its residents in aiming to create connected and sustainable communities – communities with a heart. It illustrates how key service priorities and the growth and regeneration agenda complement each other.

In telling our story then, we reveal:
* *Some of the changes and challenges* facing Kent – both as a part of south-east England confronted by significant global and national pressures, and as a county with significant social, economic and cultural differences within its boundaries; and
* *What Kent and its partners are doing to meet these challenges* – by forging partnerships and alliances across sectors, with, for example, national government, community agencies, businesses, research institutions and across all fields of expertise such as education, health, social care, employment, housing, arts and culture and commerce.

Kent background: change and growth

Strategically located between London and mainland Europe, Kent is a frontier county. With just over 1.3 million people – and experiencing a population growth of nearly 3 per cent in the ten years between 1993 and 2003 – Kent includes 2 per cent of the population of England and is bigger than 12 states in the USA. In some ways it is a microcosm of England as a whole, with much the same full range of social conditions. Resident levels of satisfaction with Kent as a place to live are exceptional (BMG, 2002).

Kent – administrative boundaries1

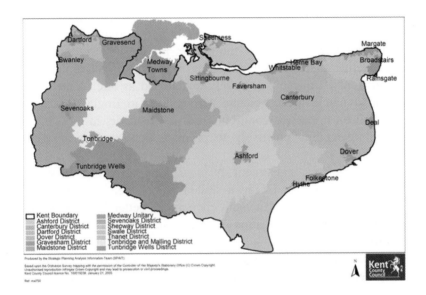

Nevertheless, Kent faces certain pressures:

- *Increasing population* – based on the current planned housing provision as outlined in the Kent and Medway Structure Plan, by 2021 it is forecast that the population of Kent will be just over 1.7 million, an increase of 121,100 people (7.7 per cent) between 2001 and 2021.
- *The changing demographics of the population*, with implications for increased demands for infrastructure such as housing, transport and education, and services such as family and child support and disability services.
- *Increased pressures on individual, family and community wellbeing* arising from the continuing and widening gap between rich and poor and the slow pace of intervention.
- *Increased demands on the tax base* combined with competing priorities and growing public expectations of government's role and capacity to intervene quickly and appropriately.
- *The changing role of local government* arising from a range of

factors including national government demands for public sector reform together with the recognition that local, community based responses are more desirable and effective than centralised service delivery mechanisms.

The Kent Partnership

The Kent Partnership is Kent's local strategic partnership, formed to enable a more effective response to the key issues facing the county. The partnership brings together key members of the public, private and voluntary sectors. Working together has, as was expected, proved more effective than working alone. The Kent Partnership is widely recognised as one of the most successful and dynamic local strategic partnerships in England. Key to that success has been the active contribution of its members in lobbying, influencing and responding positively to promote opportunities. The guiding principles are:

- *Jobs*: securing investment in new jobs, growing existing companies and developing a skilled workforce. With this last point in mind, the partnership encourages better links between employers and the education sector.
- *Infrastructure funding*: supporting the work to secure long-term infrastructure funding; identifying the county-wide funding requirement for infrastructure and public services; working together to raise funding from development land values, private finance initiatives, public/private programmes, venture capital and innovative funding streams.
- *Quality*: ensuring that developments are sustainable and of the highest quality in their design.
- *Lobbying*: presenting a unified voice for Kent in lobbying for improved rail services in the county, for example.

These principles are enshrined within and addressed by the targets in *Vision for Kent*, Kent's Community Strategy (Kent Partnership, 2002).

Kent Public Service Board and Local Area Agreement (LAA)

Existing within and accountable to the Kent Partnership is the Kent Public Service Board. Established on 29 September 2004, the Board brings together the key public sector decision-makers in the county. It is a non-statutory body, which can be characterised as the Group Board for Kent's public services, each of which continues to operate independently but spending a combined annual budget of about £7 billion.

The purpose of the Board is to support the work of the Kent Partnership in realising Kent's Community Strategy, *Vision for Kent*, and to join together the totality of public services in Kent.

The Board will address:
- the major strategic issues confronting the county and an agreed Agenda to improve the quality of life for the people of Kent;
- the development of a successful Local Area Agreement (LAA) and a second Local Public Service Agreement (LPSA2) achieved through a new form of partnership between Kent and central government;
- better coordinated direction of public services in the county with the potential to produce cutting edge improvements in service delivery for users and better value for money (VFM);
- the need for freedom from regulations and central control.

The Kent Partnership and Public Service Board are therefore leading the way in the move away from the old-fashioned linear and hierarchical approach to developing and implementing ideas, policies and programmes on a large-scale, and towards a more interactive and adaptable approach, custom-designed for smaller localities and even personalised for single individuals (Leadbeater, 2003).

Ministers and Government Spending Departments have acknowledged that the conventional machinery of national controls, targets, ring-fenced funding, inspection, audit and direct management from Whitehall are failing to deliver the improvements in public services that the public expect. Also, the difficulties of joining up government nationally have been recognised and there is a growing realisation that a new framework for local decision-making and collaboration is needed. Kent is fortunate to have been chosen as a LAA pilot. The LAA has been designed to address these issues and provides Kent with challenging three-year targets and the freedoms and flexibilities to deliver them. We have begun an exciting period of learning, experimentation and risk taking to see if together we can bring about a step change in the quality and effectiveness of all public services delivered to the people of Kent.

Kent Local Public Service Agreement (LPSA)
Contained within the LAA targets is Kent's second LPSA, LPSA2. This is a contract between Kent County Council and the national government to deliver 12 jointly selected outcomes – measurable improvements to the

quality of public services in Kent – in return for financial reward and specific freedoms and flexibilities. Some of these outcomes are county council services; some are the main responsibility of partners. Kent County Council takes on the role of prime contractor on behalf of all those agencies that have a part to play in delivering the LPSA2 targets.

LPSA targets must be 'stretching', which is to say be set to a higher standard and rate of improvement than would otherwise be the case. Targets are set around three years ahead. LPSAs are voluntary arrangements. If LPSA targets fall short, no one is any the worse off, but if the LPSA is successful, the government pays a reward grant that can be reinvested into services. Bringing together Kent County Council, partners and government with a single focus secures and delivers improved public services for the residents of Kent.

March 2004 marked the end of Kent's first three-year LPSA, LPSA1, with the national government. Ten of the 12 targets have been fully delivered triggering a Performance Reward Grant of £21.5m. According to the Office of the Deputy Prime Minister officials, Kent's result is the best of any council so far and was described as 'outstanding'. The New Local Government Network and Improvement and Development Agency placed Kent 'at the forefront of change in local government' (NLGN and IDeA, 2003) and in February 2005 Her Majesty's Treasury congratulated Kent on its LPSA1 achievements to date (Boateng, 2005). But most importantly, Kent's LPSA1 has changed people's lives for the better; services have been transformed and the level of stretch achieved has exceeded expectations[2].

Links and networks

International strategic alliances and knowledge networks are also important to Kent County Council. It is essential for Kent as a learning city region that these links are maintained and strengthened over time as a means to exchange best practice and to extend trade and tourism links where suitable opportunities can be identified.

Because of its geographical position, the county of Kent has always had a special relationship with mainland Europe, benefiting from and influencing our European neighbours. The French region of Nord Pas de Calais has collaborated with Kent County Council on European projects for more than a quarter of a century and our ties with the Hungarian county of Bacs-Kiskun are more than a decade old. A renewed memorandum of cooperation between our two counties was signed in the presence of the President of Hungary in October 2004. The Kent County Council office in Brussels is particularly active in exploring and building new relationships across Europe, especially amongst recent accession states.

Even older are the ties with the American State of Virginia, though their potential contribution to Kent has only recently been explored. The year 2007 marks the quad-centennial anniversary of the landing of the Pilgrim Fathers at Jamestown after their long transatlantic sea voyage from Deal in Kent. Historic connections with Virginia are consequently numerous and, in parallel with public awareness-raising of the forthcoming 2007 Anglo-American celebrations, new trade and learning links are being built.

New links with the Australian State of Victoria, forged through the Pascal International Observatory, will permit sharing of information on community strengthening and will inform the parallel development of Kent's new housing 'growth areas' and Victoria's own similarly designated 'transit towns'.

Promoting economic growth

There are over 55,000 businesses registered in Kent and Medway. Small businesses (up to 250 employees) account for 99 per cent of the total number of firms and create 85 per cent of new jobs. Having the right environment, support and skills to enable a dynamic small business economy is vital to the future prosperity of Kent. Kent already has a large number of strategic employment sites across the whole of the county, including the growth areas.

The *Locate in Kent* agency works to attract investment to the county. Support in this effort from central government would recognise that whilst the wider South-East continues to attract such investment without public intervention, Kent differs from that wider picture. This is partly due to perceptions (and reality) of poor transport infrastructure and to an unattractive skills mix within the Kent workforce. Both of these can be tackled by public sector intervention.

Building communities with heart: the growth and regeneration challenge

The UK government has announced a series of policies, strategies and initiatives during the last two years on housing, communities, planning, urban development, public health and homelessness (for example, DfH, 2004; HMG, 2004a, 2004b; ODPM, 2003, 2004a).

These are intended to respond to the demands of an estimated population growth of two million people per decade, much of which will be in the south-east of England. The number of first-time homebuyers is at an all-time low and they are finding it harder to take the first step onto the property ladder[3]. There are also the challenges of social change: the growth in family breakdown, later marriage, an ageing population and longer life expectancy mean more single occupation households, resulting in an ever-upward curve of demand for property. All this is happening at a time when the average number of new homes being built is also at an all-time low, according to the Government's own figures.

In 2002 the national government released its Housing Green Paper, *Quality and Choice: A Decent Home for All*, the first comprehensive review of housing for 23 years (ODPM, 2002). The Government's aim is that everyone should have the opportunity of a decent home, and that people should have a much greater involvement in, and control over, their housing choices.

Then in early 2003, through its Sustainable Communities Plan, the national government announced that housing in England would receive the significant boost of a £22bn package over three years. The government's document, *Sustainable Communities: Building for the Future*, promises 'successful, thriving and inclusive communities, urban and rural' and 'to put an end to poor housing and bad landlords, to deliver more affordable housing, especially for key workers and young families' (ODPM, 2003, foreword).

In July 2003 the Deputy Prime Minister announced proposals for funding to support and accelerate sustainable growth and housing supply in the wider South-East over the next 15 years. For Kent, this translated in the Kent Thames Gateway area to £54m funding from the Office of the Deputy Prime Minister, £28m approved and £21m amber light funding for Ashford and £23m funding for Swale for the period to 2006.

Kent County Council is clear on its objectives for Kent in the midst of these huge challenges. It wants Kent residents to have access to homes of excellent quality, in the right place, at the right time and at the right cost. To achieve this it understands the need to be creative and inventive in its approach to increasing the supply of housing that is 'affordable' to ensure that it does not simply build low-construction-cost, low-quality products that degrade our communities and degrade the quality of life for future generations.

Consequently, it has estimated that a total investment of almost £10 billion is needed across the county for the government's housing growth plans to go forward in a way that will protect and enhance Kent's:

- traditional village, rural and environmental heritage;
- commitment to excellence in design, architecture and construction to create attractive new communities;
- transport and community infrastructure; and
- employment and business sectors, with a particular focus on investing in high skills, supporting entrepreneurship and expanding business opportunities in the knowledge-economy.

These four 'Kent tests', detailed in Kent County Council's June 2003 response (KCC, 2003) to Government, underpin policies and activities, not only in the growth areas but also across the county as a whole.

Stimulating economic development

The regeneration of the Kent Thameside area will create more than 50,000 new job opportunities over the next 20 years. The Kent Thameside Delivery Board is committed to:

- securing high quality jobs for local residents; and
- developing a skilled local workforce that contributes to a successful economy.

The Board has developed a unique strategy to support these twin aims. Crucially the strategy will be employer led and tailored to the training and development needs of the local workforce (Kent Thameside Delivery Board, 2005).

Kent Thameside presents an enormous opportunity for construction industry-specific best practice training and employment programmes to be developed. The scale of the proposed developments, both in the amount of construction activity and in the length of time construction employers will be active in the area, will mean that considerable numbers of beneficiaries can be helped to develop and sustain careers in construction.

In parallel, the Kent and Medway Economic Board is working hard to develop an enterprise economy through bringing together representatives from the business community in Kent and Medway, with representatives of the public sector, economic agencies and business support organisations. The Board adds value to the work of the economic development agencies, oversees the development of a long-term economic strategy and champions its implementation, engages with the wider business community and lobbies on strategic economic issues.

Kent County Council's Economic Development Group leads the council's activities to encourage inward investment and the creation and promotion of jobs in Kent. Working in partnership with other organisations, the Economic Development Group provides high quality services to the county's business community.

It assists with the development of strategic industrial and business sites and funds *Locate in Kent*, the county's inward investment agency. It supports innovation and new technological advancement and promotes and develops tourism in Kent through the *Kent Tourism Alliance*, the county's tourism marketing agency.

Investing in transport capacity

To accommodate the planned growth in Kent it is imperative that the necessary transport infrastructure is in place early in the process. This requires a sustained programme of road and rail investment. To pay for these improvements requires the private and public sectors to work together.

A number of major transport elements must therefore be developed:

- Key connections to the trunk road network have to be improved and the capacity of the east–west A2/M2 and M20 motorways needs to be increased.
- Rail services also need to be improved so that links to and from London and between towns in Kent are faster and of better frequency and quality. The introduction of the Integrated Kent Franchise represents a unique opportunity to provide faster journeys on new trains via the Channel Tunnel Rail Link whilst maintaining an appropriate level of services to the existing London termini.
- It is essential to reduce the burden on the roads to the ports and Channel Tunnel by encouraging a shift from road to rail. There is real concern that rail services through the Tunnel will become even less competitive when the Minimum Usage Agreement ends in November 2006. Kent County Council has urged the Treasury to maintain support for international passenger and freight services to avoid more traffic on the country's main link to mainland Europe.
- Finally, London represents a serious blockage for transport

between mainland Europe and the rest of the UK, both on road and rail. Kent County Council has urgently requested the government to commission studies of the need for, and location of, a road and/or rail crossing of the Thames to the east of London.

Supporting Independence

The Supporting Independence Programme aims to help people to lift themselves out of dependency into independence and more fulfilled lives. At the same time it aims to recycle part of any benefits saving back into preventative work through education, community and social programmes. The Programme is based on the assumption that the quality of life for everyone is improved by being in work.

The Programme aims to break the spiral of deprivation by bringing partner agencies together to target local communities where there is a clear need. Therefore the challenge of Supporting Independence is to create 'joined-up' systems, which enable families and individuals, sometimes in the poorest parts of Kent, to access worthwhile training and fulfilling jobs. Many of the LPSA1 and LPSA2 targets are very specifically aimed at delivering Supporting Independence Programme outcomes.

Supporting healthy communities

The role of enabling people to maintain and protect their health has too often been regarded as predominantly the remit of the National Health Service, with the role of local authorities undervalued. In the context of managing the growth agenda, transport, regeneration and housing can each have a far greater impact upon public health than the usual activities that are funded under a public health label.

Successful management of the growth agenda demands that Kent County Council and its local partners meet the challenge of ensuring that rapid growth impacts positively on the health of the people of Kent. New communities must be planned, and existing communities invested in, in order that residents' opportunities to walk and cycle, to access leisure facilities, to buy healthy food and to keep warm in winter are maximised. The scale of new development offers an unprecedented opportunity to design health into the new communities that are being planned, thereby claiming a significant health dividend for Kent residents.

This approach is consistent with the 'fully engaged' public health scenario set out in the Wanless Report (Wanless, 2002). However, if local government is to be encouraged to take on a responsibility for preventing downstream health problems, then this must be reflected in national assessment regimes and local governance arrangements.

The *Smart Village* concept is being developed to input to the development of healthy communities. The village is a micro-community of 500–1500 people that celebrates the best in twenty-first century living and working. It is unique in combining innovative technology and first-rate contemporary design with the friendly culture and traditions of the Kent village.

It will be:
- *Supportive* – a safe, democratic community, home to people from all walks of life who have the confidence, capacity and skills not only to shape the well-being of their own community but also to influence others across Britain and beyond.
- *Healthy and fun* – close to great countryside and leisure/cultural activities, to ensure individual and community well-being across all age groups.
- *Environmentally responsible* – developing innovative technologies in design, construction and maintenance to ensure minimal use of energy and resources.
- *Economically vibrant* – home to the twenty-first century bioscience, creative and digital industries, linked into education and training provision, and an energetic participant in local and global economic networks.

The *Smart Village* concept is testament to the fact that we want Kent to be a balanced community, which grows as a whole without excluding sections of society, and which creates opportunities for all.

More broadly, the choice of housing options in Kent must be significantly increased to attract those desiring to be part of an inclusive and supportive society. Housing – either newly constructed or existing stock – must also, logically, be priced within the financial means of Kent residents.

The role of the private sector in the housing market then is critical to achieving our aims of creating and sustaining the supply of excellent housing in Kent. We are working to encourage enterprise and support risk in the private market by identifying joint investment opportunities, and also to enhance the private sector's capacity to develop the extensive supply of land already allocated for housing.

Improving quality of life for all

The support and help that families need differs from family to family; it is therefore crucial that new and existing communities have a wide range of support services available to them. If families are helped and supported, the effects and causes of poverty and family breakdown can be tackled.

Providing support and promoting prevention, earlier rather than later when the difficulties have become ingrained, is the most effective response with the greatest impact and chance of success. This is evidenced by studies such as the USA Headstart Longitudinal Studies[4]. Ideally this will be delivered within the community where families are based.

In response to the growth agenda and within the context of the newly developed national Preventative Strategy for Children (DfES, 2003), we are:
- establishing more community-based family support services, focused on communities in need, which harness the strengths within family networks and the community. This includes:
  - extending schemes such as Play Link[5], Home Start[6], High Scope[7], the Link Family Scheme[8] and Sure Start[9] across Kent;
  - extending family group conferencing;
  - supporting the voluntary sector to access external funding for family support schemes;
- ensuring a coordinated programme of support for children in need by developing a closer relationship with pre-school services, early years education and the voluntary sector, ensuring early help is identified and available.

Many older people lead active, full lives and make an enormous (yet often unrecognised) contribution to society. Many older people are carers or heavily involved in voluntary community activities. To develop their full potential they need more easily accessible leisure activity, employment and volunteering opportunities.

Housing has a huge impact on an older person's quality of life. People who, in the past, would almost certainly have been in residential care are increasingly able to retain a large degree of independence if they live in well-designed and appropriately-supported accommodation. For example, people who become more frail as they get older can stay at home much longer if that home has no stairs (or can take a stairlift), has a bathroom big enough for a wheelchair to turn in, wide doors and appropriate equipment to live at home safely.

In addition, Kent is leading the way in implementing Assistive Technology, or Telecare. This is the new generation of equipment following on from the more familiar lifeline pendants and alarms that many older and disabled people are using in their homes already.

When an alarm is triggered, whether by a smoke or flood detector, a bogus caller alarm or a falls detector for example, a call goes through to a monitoring centre. Call operators try to speak to the service user and alert the appropriate response. This may involve calling on any of a range of people, from the carer of the service user, a neighbour or, if necessary, the emergency services.

Strong evidence from elsewhere suggests that, if complemented by the right infrastructure and support services, this technology can be used as a tool to help reduce pressure on scarce staff, reduce admissions to hospital and residential care, and contribute towards the reduction of delayed discharges from hospital.

Most importantly it can increase choice and control for vulnerable people and their carers, increase the dignity of vulnerable people and thus reduce their fear of being a burden.

In Kent we embarked on a six-month pilot scheme in July 2004 in three districts – Swale, Maidstone, and Tonbridge and Malling, involving 50 house-holds in each district.

Learning in Kent

A Kent community school should be a focal point for a range of educational, cultural, sport, family and community services. The aim is to make a range of services more accessible, better coordinated and more driven by the needs of those they serve. There may be opportunities for new, integrated approaches to childcare, family learning and support services, adult education linked to the 16–19 curriculum and business-based vocational training. It is about involving the community more in the life of the school and the school in the life of the community, in order to enrich both.

As part of our vision of community schools, we also welcome start-up companies on school sites to promote the enterprise culture, engage employers and bring business into the classroom – and the classroom into business.

In line with the aim of diversity in learning, Kent has developed a dynamic and visionary 14–19 Strategy, drawn up in partnership by Kent County Council, the local Learning and Skills Council[10] and Connexions[11]. At the heart of this strategy and the action plan that accompanies it is a determination for these three partners to collaborate to raise achievement and provide an excellent curriculum tailored to the needs of each individual. Vocational education is central to making this happen.

Kent's unique contribution to advancing the vocational agenda is to commit £6 million in a three-year capital programme to build the first phase of a series of state-of-the-art applied vocational centres for 14–16 year-old school students. Located on or near school sites, these centres offer a varied and complementary vocational programme that should appeal to young people of all abilities. Centres within a given area are open to young people of all neighbouring schools. All students are working towards recognised and valued vocational qualifications. Links with local employers are being developed. Students will progress from these centres to apprenticeships, further education[12], foundation degrees[13] and employment.

Furthermore, Kent County Council puts pupils and their families in direct control of their own learning. For example, Kent has engineered the UK's largest deployment of Tablet PCs into the education system. Kent County Council has partnered with Microsoft, transforming the teaching process and dramatically improving productivity. Each tablet is wireless, the size of a book, and can be used in the classroom, home or elsewhere. It is capable of storing all source material and student work for an entire academic year and beyond.

Safeguarding environmental heritage

Kent's environmental heritage is a key element of what makes Kent an attractive location for businesses and is central to residents' perceptions of their quality of life. Developing urban green space, links to public rights of way and other 'green infrastructure' are all important elements of the environmental quality that we are seeking.

The Kent Environment Strategy commits us to:

- recognise the importance of the environment on the doorstep to communities' health and sense of well being;
- sustain the countryside as a prosperous rural economy, with vibrant and well-served communities, for the benefit of Kent's rural and urban dwellers alike;
- increase access to, and understanding of, Kent's historic heritage, and safeguard this so that existing and new residents of Kent may benefit;
- manage the waste produced by an enlarged population and maximise opportunities for recycling and composting in new residential developments.

The housing growth figures in Kent represent a significant increase in the demand for certain resources, notably water and energy. In the case of water, Kent is one of the driest counties in the country. It already has some areas where water is over-abstracted. Despite recent progress in reducing leakage from water supply infrastructure, water consumption per capita continues to rise and the UK performs poorly in terms of water-use efficiency.

Significant reductions in water use are possible with existing, proven technology. The new housing growth areas represent an opportunity to incorporate such measures, deferring the need for more expensive investments on the supply side.

In a recent Kent County Council study (Butters, Lockie and Fenner, 2003) of the whole-life costing of a number of schools, we identified that investment in the environmental performance of the building represented good value for money over the longer term. Government support has been requested to ensure that this forms the basis of an *Invest to Save* approach in the future commissioning and funding of new school buildings.

Nurturing creativity

Kent County Council recognises its responsibility to encourage and support the vast creative potential of the people of Kent. Creative thinkers in every profession from science, industry, business and marketing, to the public and voluntary sectors emerge from an environment that is characterised by a creative culture.

Key to making this real is widening access across ages, ethnicity and social groups. Promoting mixed-use buildings and developments, which include space for arts and other cultural activity, is one potential means of addressing this. Any aspiration to raise the level of cultural and creative activity in Kent needs to be accompanied by an understanding of potential 'consumers', who will be drawn from among both residents and visitors.

The investment in *Turner Contemporary*, Kent's new international arts organisation, reflects this powerful opportunity. The project has two principal objectives: (i) to provide a major visual arts venue, which will (ii) provide a catalyst for the regeneration of Margate, where it is based, and East Kent. The project arose from within the community – Margate Civic Society – and has firm local roots. The community wanted to find a way to celebrate the town's very strong associations with Britain's best-loved painter. J.M.W. Turner first visited Margate as a young boy and later became a resident of the town that he loved for the sea and the skies. The essential leadership for this £25m capital project in Margate has been provided by the county council, although it will be funded by a broad partnership and the gallery will be operated by an independent charitable Trust.

The commitment to a *Creative Quarter* as a key to the regeneration of the seaside town of Folkestone also points to a strong intent to build on Kent's cultural heritage and step out in contemporary spheres.

Transforming existing public services such as libraries also has a role to play in promoting creativity and stimulating learning. The concept of *Discovery Centres* provides the physical infrastructure within which this transformation can take place. Central government support for Kent County Council's Ashford Discovery Centre needs to be replicated for the programme as a whole across Kent.

The Ashford Discovery Centre will be a landmark building situated in a prime town centre location. It will act as a hub for the newly-emergent town centre, bringing together high quality materials and cutting edge technology to create a magnet both for the community and for inward investment. The Discovery Centre will make a major contribution to Ashford's growth area agenda by becoming an exemplar of quality and innovation, thus setting the standard for future development. The provision, in the short term, of such a building will be instrumental to the unlocking of development potential in the town centre. Every aspect from the design of the building to the purpose that it will serve is in line with the aspirations for the growth area as a whole.

Promoting design excellence

The criteria for success of the expansion of buildings and creativity in Kent will not only be governed by prestigious one-off projects or even the numbers of houses built. It will be about the quality of the places created. Development on this scale brings with it an opportunity for a step-change in the quality of the houses we build in the county, the attractiveness of the communities we create and the vitality of our towns and villages. The new Kent Design Guide places high quality design at the heart of the decision-making process.

Kent Design is a unique initiative, bringing together the public and private sectors in the push for better planning and design. The new guide is a thorough overhaul of *Kent Design – A Guide to Sustainable Development* (Kent Association of Local Authorities, 2000). This latter document was highly praised for its ground-breaking approach, and since its publication in 2000 many new buildings in Kent have met the very highest standards. The 2005 Guide is being adopted by the Local Planning Authorities as a Supplementary Planning Document, so can be a material consideration in determining planning applications and thereby play a key role in determining the nature of future development.

In order to champion good design and produce memorable buildings that are relevant to the county, Kent County Council has given the role of Kent Design Champion to Piers Gough, one of Britain's leading architects. *The Guardian* national newspaper reported this as:

> a bold move, given Gough's outspoken views and his un-shakeable enthusiasm for uncompromising modern architecture typified by his controversial futuristic plan for Hove's seafront,

designed in partnership with architectural superstar Frank Gehry, designer of Bilbao's Guggenheim museum.

In Kent, though, Gough will be championing careful urban planning rather than showy icons. It is his daunting task to encourage sustainable, attractive high quality developments in the Thames Gateway, the principal site of the government's massive house building plan for the South-East (about which his council employers are distinctly nervous). (Morris, 2004)

Also part of the Kent Design initiative is Kent's Building Design Awards, held annually to reward excellence in the field of building, public space, community design and regeneration in Kent.

There are more questions than answers

What this chapter sets out is very much only the story so far. We feel that we have begun to create a clear, shared and widely acknowledged account of the challenges. We have found or created new ways of working and new products that we are confident will contribute to achieving our ambitions. Much of this is untested; in some cases we are still getting to grips with the scale and nature of these challenges. There is much to be done in working with those partners on whom we will rely for delivery and we have not reached the point where we are certain of the way ahead.

For example:
- How can we move from being the regulator of growth to a genuine partner of the development industry?
- What tools can we use not only to bridge the skills gap for future generations, but also to act on the needs of employers from the workforce of today?
- How do we work with local communities to overcome their reluctance to accept change and recognise the benefits that growth and regeneration can bring?
- Is the emphasis we put on high quality design and place-making justified?

Kent is a great place to live, work and visit. Our challenge is to make a great place even better. We would welcome ideas, suggestions and contributions from anywhere else in the world to help us create a better Kent.

Correspondence: Any correspondence should be directed to Dr Alison St.Clair Baker, Kent County Council, Invicta House, Maidstone, Kent, ME14 1XX (alison.stclairbaker@kent.gov.uk).

Notes

[1] Kent operates a two-tier local government system with county and district councils. Kent County Council has been under Conservative administration since 1997 under the leadership of Sir Sandy Bruce-Lockhart, who is also Chair of the UK Local Government Association.

[2] Some LPSA targets include:

- *Adoptions*: Kent now has the highest rate of adoptions in the country, having trebled the number over a three-year period.
- *Looked-after Children*: the enormous reduction in the number of children in care (over 20 per cent) is even more remarkable in the interest of a strong upward national trend.
- *Hospital Discharges and Residential Care*: by working with health and introducing a range of innovative programmes, substantially more elderly people were provided with services enabling them to stay in their own homes.
- *Young Offenders*: the prevention of reconviction of a large number of the 'hardest to reach' young people involved using a radical programme of diversionary activities and largely intensive support.
- *Public Disorder*: incidents of public disorder have been reduced by almost 30 per cent, through working with the police and other partners and by focusing on known problem areas.

[3] The housing shortage in the south-east of England has forced up house prices by an estimated 70 per cent between 1999 and 2003, according to the recent *South East Regional Housing Strategy*, which calls for significant investment to tackle the shortage of high-quality, affordable homes.

[4] USA Project Head Start, launched as an eight-week summer program by the Office of Economic Opportunity in 1965, was designed to help break the cycle of poverty by providing preschool children of low-income families with a comprehensive programme to meet their emotional, social, health, nutritional, and psychological needs.

[5] Playlink is a not-for-profit organisation supporting local authorities, organisations and groups that want to create the best possible play opportunities for children and young people. Playlink offers advice, information and services related to creating sustainable quality play environments.

[6] Home-Start is the UK's leading family support charity. Home-Start's informal and friendly support for families with young children provides a lifeline to thousands of

parents and children in over 337 communities across the UK and with forces families in Germany and Cyprus.

[7] High/Scope UK exists to foster the betterment of young children's lives and consequent life chances through a high quality education programme which is underpinned by proven long-term research and called the High/Scope Curriculum.

[8] The Kent County Council Link Scheme provides short breaks for children of all ages, from infants to 19 year olds with disabilities of all kinds including severe learning disabilities, physical, visual or hearing impairments and chronic medical conditions.

[9] Sure Start in the UK is based on the USA's Head Start programme. Kent has benefited greatly from all these provisions with a trailblazer Sure Start scheme in Thanet, followed by Dover, Shepway and Swale.

[10] The Learning Skills Council, launched in April 2001, is responsible for the planning and funding of all post-16 education and training in the county, except for higher education.

[11] Connexions is the government's support service for all young people aged 13 to 19 in England – see www.connexionskentandmedway.co.uk for details of the local service.

[12] Further education is for people over compulsory school age (currently 16 in England), which does not take place in a secondary school. It may be in a sixth-form college, a further education college or a higher education institution. Further education courses are generally up to the standard of GCE A-level or NVQ Level 3.

[13] A vocational degree takes two years full-time or three years if taken as a sandwich course. A foundation degree can lead straight on to an honours first degree, which could be completed in twelve months. Entry requirements are at least one A-level (or equivalent) or a vocational qualification at level 3, e.g. NVQ.

Chapter 9

South Africa's Learning Cape aspirations: the idea of a learning region and the use of indicators in a middle-income country

Shirley Walters
Director, Division for Lifelong Learning, University of Western Cape, South Africa

Make every home, every shack or rickety structure a centre of learning.

Nelson Mandela

Introduction

The main questions with which this chapter grapples are: can lower or middle-income countries become or contain learning regions? Is lifelong learning suitable only for richer nations or regions? Is it possible for a province like the Western Cape Province in South Africa, which represents vast disparities between people who are rich and poor, black and white, to be a learning region? Is there any point in the Province aspiring to become a learning region?

These are real questions that confront those working on the ground in the Province on a daily basis. It is too early to give authoritative answers to these questions. Many people are immersed in complex social and institutional processes and attempting under difficult circumstances to imagine the province as a learning region. This paper is presented as a preliminary reflective dialogue, and a way of identifying some of the critical issues. I write as a participant observer, who has been closely involved in various aspects of the Learning Cape, including being invited to critique early drafts of the provincial government's White Paper on the Knowledge Economy (PAWC, 2001), being commissioned to write a working paper on 'Developing the Learning Cape' (Division for Lifelong Learning, 2001), chairing the Learning Cape Festival's Steering Committee for the last four years and undertaking research for the Learning Indicators Project (DLL/ODA, 2005).

The Western Cape Province is one of the nine provinces of South Africa. It aspires to being a learning province, called the Learning Cape. This account locates the developments historically, describes the competing understandings of the Learning Cape and analyses two strategies that are illustrative of attempts to engage seriously with the concept. They are the Learning Cape Festival, which is in its fourth year, and the Learning Cape Indicators Project, which has drafted preliminary indicators. The chapter ends with a reflective dialogue.

A learning region and its characteristics

I have argued elsewhere that there seem to be certain essential characteristics of a learning region (Walters, 2005a). These include: world-class education and training systems at all levels, with high participation rates; high levels of collaboration, networking and clustering within and across economic and knowledge sectors, especially around areas of innovation; world-class systems for collection, analysis, management and dissemination of information; constant challenging of traditional knowledge categories to suit rapidly changing social and economic realities; the provision of frequently updated, easily-accessible information and counselling services to enable citizens to maximise their learning opportunities; high value placed on formal, non-formal and informal learning throughout life expressed in tangible improvements in the learner's employment and community situations; and learning support for high levels of social cohesion across social class, ethnicity, gender, ability, geography and age within a society of limited social polarities. There is an assumption (supported by European Union strategies) that countries will not be able to move to competitive knowledge economies if there is not sufficient social cohesion.

Most of the countries developing the concept of learning regions are high-income countries. However, in middle-income countries like Brazil, India and South Africa, the challenge is to interpret and develop the notion in contexts of widespread poverty and social polarisation. Some regions may emphasise high-end research and development for economic development. Others may also highlight the importance of social justice and equity as integral to economic success. In the next section a sketch is provided of the aspirant Learning Cape.

The Learning Cape

Situating the `Learning Cape` within national debates

South Africa re-entered the global economy just over a decade ago after a sustained period of exclusion. At the same time, the new government expressed its inevitable commitment (given South Africa's history) to equity and redress in a Reconstruction and Development Programme. Since then, the central debate has been around the nature of South Africa's insertion into the global economy, with some advocating a high-end ICT focus and others seeking more directly to channel the forces of globalisation for the elimination of poverty (for example, Daniel et al., 2003).

This debate, together with material conditions expressed by an unemployment rate between 30 and 40 per cent, and general agreement that the country's skills deficit is a key limiting factor, represents the context for human development (HSRC, 2003).

The Regional Context

The Western Cape is the second wealthiest province in South Africa. On the one hand, certain parts of the economy are fairly buoyant, like tourism, services for film, media and IT, and the fruit and wine industry. On the other hand, 65 per cent of people earn below US $200 per month, there is 26 per cent unemployment, 30 per cent of adults are 'illiterate', 78 per cent of preschoolers do not have access to early childhood development opportunities and the number of tuberculosis and HIV/Aids infected people is increasing rapidly. The disparities between rich and poor are among the most extreme in the world.

A brief picture of the Province emerges from the following data:

GDPR   Primary industry 5.4%, Secondary 24.1%, tertiary 61.6%

                  Since 1995 the primary and secondary share has decreased by 5% (Western Cape Provincial Territory, 2003)

Population age   67.5% of working age (15 to 65 years) (Statistics South Africa, 2001)

Income   67% of wage earners earned below the poverty line (Provincial Department of Social Services and Poverty Alleviation, 2005, p. 11)

42% of households had annual income of less than US$3,000 (Statistics South Africa, 2001)

Education

Level of Schooling	2001 (%)
No schooling	5.7
Some Primary	15.2
Completed Primary	7.9
Some Secondary	36.5
Grade 12	23.4
Higher	11.2
Total	*100*

Source: Adapted from Western Cape Provincial Treasury (2005, p. 61), based on Statistics SA Census 2001

ECD   22% of under-fives attend an early childhood centre (Provincial Department of Social Services and Poverty Alleviation, 2005, p. 14)

HIV/Aids   Incidence of 12.4% (Provincial Department of Social Services and Poverty Alleviation, 2005, pp. 13–17)

Children   Social Services currently has 4,400 cases of child abuse on their books, know of 780 street children and report an average 2,223 youth arrested per month (Provincial Department of Social Services and Poverty Alleviation, 2005, pp. 13–17)

Further and higher education   Four Higher Education Institutions (national competence)

Six Further Education and Training (FET) colleges (provincial competence), each with a number of campuses

The key socio-economic statistics for the Province illustrate its divisions:

26 per cent unemployment (Statistics South Africa, 2001) breaks down as:

- 41 per cent for black African and 6.9 per cent for whites (Provincial Department of Social Services and Poverty Alleviation, 2005, p. 10)
- 46 per cent of age group 16–25 years (only 17 per cent of the employment market) (Western Cape Provisional Treasury, 2005, p. 8)
- The majority of white 17–year-olds and coloured 19–year-olds, but less than 30 per cent of black Africans, had ever worked (Western Cape Provisional Treasury, 2003, p. 50)
- 51 per cent of employed people earn less than US$200 per month while 5 per cent earn more than US$1900 (Statistics South Africa, 2001)
- Estimates are that 75 per cent of white new labour market entrants will get jobs compared with 29 per cent of black Africans (HSRC, 2003)
- Infant mortality in the South Peninsula (middle class) is 13 per 1,000 live births; in Khayelitsha (working class) it is 44 per 1,000

In terms of the characteristics of a learning region, we can assume that with these extremities the attainment of social cohesion would be extremely difficult.

The Learning Cape framework

In 2001 the provincial government, after lengthy consultative processes, adopted an economic development White Paper (PAWC, 2001) that argued for an intimate relationship between economic development and learning within a learning-region framework, coining the term Learning Cape, as one of four key pillars for economic and social development. The White Paper set out to address the 'twin challenges of increasing competitiveness and alleviating poverty in the global knowledge economy of the 21st century'. Since then economic development strategies have been developed further, but without the same explicit reference to the language of the Learning Cape.

Whilst the use of the Learning Cape framework is not yet entrenched as a foundation of government policy, the Learning Cape concept and preliminary moves being made to develop it in a systematic way represent the most explicit and determined example of serious engagement with the notion of the learning society in South Africa (Walters, 2005b).

Illustrative strategies towards the Learning Cape

Learning Cape Festival (LCF)

In October 2001 there was a proposal to the Provincial Department of Economic Development (DED) from the University of the Western Cape that an annual Learning Cape Festival could contribute to the development of the concept and strategy of the Learning Cape. DED canvassed the proposal amongst higher education, civil society, trade unions, business, local government, libraries and the Department of Education. A Steering Committee made up of the range of social partners from government, trade unions, higher education, early childhood, schooling, adult basic education, NGOs and Sector Education and Training Authorities (SETAs) was set up to run it. A series of theme groups was also established. Starting the month-long festival on National Women's Day, 9 August, and ending it on International Literacy Day, 8 September, it was hoped that some of the issues of the most marginalised citizens would be profiled in the festival.

Since then there have been three month-long festivals in 2002, 2003 and 2004, with a fourth planned for 2005. I will not attempt to do justice here to the depth, breadth and texture of the month's 500 or more activities, but discuss some pockets of intense engagement which illustrate how the festival's promoted various forms of learning, advocacy, networking and partnership-building within and across sectors (Walters and Etkind, 2004):

- Two community workers in a poor, working-class, gang-dominated township used the festival as a way of promoting its sustainable community projects. The festival provided a rare, conflict-free space: 'everyone could agree on the importance of building a lifelong learning culture'. It linked programmes on adult literacy, early childhood development, health, science (in partnership with higher education), small business skills development, sports and recreation, and second chance learning with both personal (individual) and community (collective) development, as well as promoting local citizen actions to the broader Cape Town community.
- A pioneering, collaborative exercise of the four Higher Education Institutions (HEIs) led to a standing committee to explore links between HEIs and the Learning Cape initiative.
- The LCF was influential in the establishment by the Provincial Departments of Economic Affairs and Education of a process that produced a framework for human resource development strategy for the Province, and participated in its activities. It stressed the

significance of linkages and partnerships within a learning province framework.

In summary, using Coffield's (2000) framework, the LCF has helped to move ideas of lifelong learning beyond 'romance' to 'evidence' and 'implementation'. It has profiled lifelong learning that is concerned with economic development and social equity and redress. This has been possible because of the particular socio-economic imperatives in the area, but also because of the composition of the Steering Committee, which has had fairly strong civil society and government representation, but weak participation from business. Implementation has reached the stage of establishing a non-governmental organisation (NGO) structure, bringing together the four social partners, business, government, labour and civil society, plus higher education, the Sector Education and Training Authorities, and the LCF Steering Committee called the Learning Cape Initiative.

The LCF has highlighted in important ways that to work out of silos takes practice. It requires people who can facilitate the processes, which key into important issues for the different sectors. It takes long-term vision and sustained commitment to working together. It is interesting to note that the City Development Strategies[1] have a timeframe of 30 years, which seems more realistic than the dominant short-term development cycles. It requires ongoing advocacy to motivate and to mobilise resources to support the activities. These have captured the imagination of many people and given hope that creating a learning region may be possible, with enormous potential to be a vehicle for institutions and individuals to learn to behave differently. Trust has been built amongst a diverse set of practitioners and institutions. It is, however, very fragile and requires constant vigilance in order that one sector, institution or individual does not dominate and so render others passive.

Indicators of success for the Learning Cape

Recommendation one of the HRDS Framework Report (PAWC 2003, p. 42), focusing on Benchmarks for a Learning Cape, states that:

> it is necessary to set targets and develop indicators for measuring and monitoring progress towards the Learning Cape, which include socio-economic indicators and those relating to the quality of education and training. The indicators are to help stakeholder organizations, sectors and the learning province as a whole to measure and to monitor progress and performance.

Monitoring would be done continuously with annual public accounting of progress reported to all stakeholders.

Influenced by this recommendation, the provincial DED set up a preliminary research and development project 'to develop Learning Cape Indicators'. Together with colleagues from the Organisation for Development in Africa (ODA) and Division for Lifelong Learning, I undertook a limited, four-month project now under way. Several pertinent issues have been raised which will inform this discussion.

What are indicators and what is their purpose?

We worked on the understanding that an indicator is a measure requiring data that helps quantify the achievement of a desired result (DLL/ODA, 2005). Indicators help answer the question how we would know a result if we achieved it. Taken further, indicators can play a key role in policy development:

> At their most noble, civic indicators are used as measuring systems to assist societies and communities towards a desired course, to clarify key issues and challenges, and to prioritise resources, especially spending. They do not just monitor progress; they help make it happen. (Reed, 2000)

What is a learning indicator?

The task was to develop *learning* indicators, not indicators of 'education and training'. This expresses the broad lifelong learning focus of the exercise, away from an emphasis on formal education and towards the informal and non-formal.

To capture the centrality of the relationship of learning to economic and social development, we drew on Belanger's (1994) work, which circumscribed three broad areas that are interlinked and represent the life cycle and the learning contexts. They are:

Initial Learning, including non-formal learning of children from birth, and schooling at general and further educational levels;

Adult Learning, including ABET and higher and continuing education throughout adult life until death; and

Diffuse Learning Environments, which are enhanced through the educational quality of libraries, the media, cultural activities, learning cultures in families, voluntary associations and so on.

The approach which we adopted was to start with the characteristics, as described earlier on page 129, which reinforce the Provincial Premier's commitment to entrench a 'culture of social dialogue' in the attainment of economic development and social cohesion. We accepted that in order to have a learning region there is need of 'an excellent education and training system', without subscribing to the view that there is a linear process whereby the existence of an excellent formal system must precede any attempt to develop a broader informal and non-formal learning culture. There is ample evidence that an excellent formal system is not possible without facilitative learning cultures in families, workplaces and communities. This led us to identify the formal education system as part of the bedrock of a learning region and a set of 'bedrock indicators' for which different parts of the formal education system are responsible. These act as a backdrop to the more specific, unique Learning Cape indicators.

We also recognised that development of learning indicators was not a politically neutral process. As Duke (2004) points out, in the international literature on learning neighbourhoods, communities, cities and regions, there are important differences of purpose and priority, as well as different ways of going about policy interventions. The commonest tensions are between economic and social dimensions and between the individual and the collective. Economic purposes are sometimes interpreted and sought in individual terms such as job acquisition and reduced unemployment levels, or the acquisition and accreditation of skills thought necessary to gain employment and match labour market needs. Another approach is to consider the economic character of a community in its locality and to look for indicators of rising prosperity such as employment, productivity, mobility of skilled labour and inward capital investment. In one case the individuals and their collective achievements are the focus of attention; the other focuses on the achievement of particular communities. Underpinning the particular approaches are understandings of economic and social development. Some stress the importance of social indicators like those of health and social welfare, while others will specifically highlight economic indicators. In all cases the intention is to create a sufficient upward spiral to enable economic and social development.

Background research highlighted the fact that indicator construction is a social process. It requires consultation and is therefore slow. The process was seen as being able to be used to win supporters for the Learning Cape Initiative and to spread the discussion within the province on how to promote a learning region and learning communities.

Envisaged sites for developing indicators of the Learning Cape

We developed a matrix to draw together chronological and locational aspects of learning:

Categories for indicators

↓ →	Formal	Informal	Non-formal
Initial Learning	General education	Family	Early childhood development
		Friends	
	Further education		
		Communities	
Adult Learning	ABET	Family	Workplace
	Workplace learning	Friends	Parenting
		Work colleagues	Literacy
	Higher education		
		Community organisations	Language
	Trade union education		Trade unions
			Government
Diffuse Learning Environments		Community events	Civil society organisations
		Media	– Faith-based
		Libraries	– Environmental
		Arts and culture	– Health
		Internet	

Since every sector potentially has its own form of indicators and measures to evaluate progress, we operated on the assumption that what makes the

Learning Cape indicators unique is the combination of indicators across the sectors and how they relate to the summary of characteristics of a learning province. Our methodology deliberately left open the possibility for other parts of the provincial government, other spheres of government or organisations of civil society to sponsor data baskets.

Foundation (Bedrock) Indicators

Using the three organising categories of initial, adult and diffuse, a cluster of indicators was identified from the initial and adult categories that form the foundation of a learning region. As the bedrock of learning, a positive assessment of these indicators is essential to the development of lifelong learning in the region. These indicators are mainly but not solely the responsibility of the Western Cape Education Department and National Department of Education. An illustrative sample of these indicators, from PAWC (2005), are:

Initial learning

1. Proportion of children aged 0–4 attending Early Childhood Development (ECD)
2. Proportion of Grade 3, 6 and 9 learners who score above the target level for numeracy and literacy
3. Proportion of learners who enter the system in Grade 1 compared to the proportion of learners who exit the system in Grade 12
4. Number of computers per learner in public schools

Adult learning

1. Improvement in the throughput rate in Further Education and Training (FET) colleges
2. Improvement in the level of enrolment of ABET learners in Level 1–4 exams

Sources of data for the bedrock indicators are mostly available through statistics within the Department of Education.

The bigger challenge was to imagine the indicators that would be more specific to the Learning Cape and less reflective of mainstream education.

Proposed Learning Cape Indicators

In order to decide on these indicators, the 'essential characteristics of a learning region' were used, with the three lifelong learning categories. Thirty-four indicators were developed and reflected against the characteristics. A sample of the indicators is given below:

Initial learning

Indicator

1   Effective functioning of an ECD inter-sectoral group in province
2   Proportion of children recognised as vulnerable
3   Use of school facilities for public events related to learning

Adult learning

Indicator

1   Proportion of learners in FET colleges over 24 years of age
2   Increase in resourcing of ABET by province and workplaces
3   A rise in absolute numbers and proportion of employees in skilled categories of work and a fall in the numbers and proportion in the unskilled category 'elementary occupations'.
4   Extent to which HEIs help to stimulate innovation and knowledge transfer between researchers and industry

Diffuse learning environments

Indicator

1   Number of municipalities that actively promote involvement in the annual Learning Cape Festival
2   The number of computers, in working order, that are in libraries and linked to the internet or searchable databases (excluding the library catalogue) per citizen
3   Percentage of educational programmes on local radio

Attempting to decide on Learning Cape indicators opens a host of difficult issues. One of the challenges is to work with people coming out of different traditions and professional fields, with different and competing understandings. To illustrate this I use a brief example of children under the age of 5[2].

The proposed indicators were:
- proportion of children aged 0–4 attending an early childhood facility;
- proportion of children recognised as vulnerable in terms of their weight, cognitive and physical development, HIV/Aids status or poverty level.

Given the scenario that less than 22 per cent of the under-five population currently attend an early childhood facility and that 42 per cent of the households in the Western Cape have an annual income below $3,000, these seemed to be potentially useful indicators. The researchers argued that there was in all likelihood a relationship between improving socio-economic conditions and improving educational opportunities.

The initial response from one economist was that 'five-year-old children had nothing to do with the economy'. Another response was from the marginal early childhood facility sector which was thrilled to have the connection between early childhood facility and the socio-economic conditions recognised. Yet another was from a person in the Department of Social Services who stressed how important it was for the government to see the 'whole child' when developing policies for children. Supporters of lifelong learning continually stressed the importance of early learning experiences in terms of developing lifelong learners who would eventually be able to contribute successfully to the economy and society more broadly. It was a working mother who most clearly pointed out the real benefit, in her view, of good early childhood education. It was to free her up to rejoin the workforce. The economists were persuaded on hearing this. The indicator was retained for the time being.

Another major concern related to the processes of development of the indicators. There had been an initial intention to produce the preliminary indicators through participatory processes, but this was short-circuited because of unfolding economic policy developments. In the midst of the process, there was pressure from the DED to make the indicators more obviously connected to the emerging micro-economic development strategy. So starting from a broad approach there were signals to narrow down.

The tensions described earlier, which reflect the national debates, were also apparent provincially. Certain economists began to ask for more conventional, internationally comparable, economic and human development data. Others could see the importance of trying to cover new developmental ground. The researchers began also to see the vastness of the project, which needed to establish legitimacy for new indicators for which there were no ready data. Those leading in the Department of Economic Development would not necessarily see their role as leading innovators thinking about the learning region and the role of lifelong learning in it. This begs the question, where should a cross-cutting project like this be housed? The indicators project is not yet final and the use to which the indicators will be put is not clear.

Emerging questions
The Indicators project raised many questions beyond the indicators themselves and their use. It raised the issue of the conceptual framework for

understanding the learning region from a lifelong learning perspective. It posed questions of how to measure lifelong learning and who is responsible for it. It challenged the thinking and practices of government departments to move 'out of their silos' while illustrating the contests over turf that exist. The different tiers of government, local, provincial and national, each have their own relationships to the State and the economy, each with their own rules. It highlighted problems with available data and how this availability can pull the indicators towards formal education and training. Moving out of silos and into partnerships means that institutions have to confront these tensions. There is need for extensive social processes to change deeply entrenched behaviours. There needs to be a long-term commitment to building the vision and the practices of a learning region.

Discussion and Conclusions

Key questions posed at the outset were: can lower or middle-income countries become learning regions or is lifelong learning suitable only for richer nations or regions? Is it possible for a province like the Western Cape Province in South Africa, which represents vast disparities between people who are rich and poor, black and white, to be a learning region? Is there any point in the Province aspiring to become a learning region?

These are real questions that confront those working on the ground in the Province on a daily basis. I conclude by enjoining these questions through a preliminary reflective dialogue with a colleague[3] as a way of bringing together some critical issues.

SW: There are such wide disparities within our society, I cannot see in the foreseeable future how attainment of a learning region is possible if we accept the 'essential characteristics' as spelt out.

ON: I agree. If we look at the state of formal education and training, which is the bedrock of the learning region, we have a long way to go. The state of our data in order to monitor developments is also questionable. Then the enormous polarities around social class, race, gender and geography, which exacerbate violence and crime, don't make me optimistic that high degrees of social cohesion are likely any time soon. I reckon that, like real democracy itself, the Learning Cape will remain aspirational, something towards which to strive.

SW: The framework of lifelong learning has been projected nationally within policy frameworks. It has been largely symbolic except for the important innovation of the National Qualifications Framework. The Learning Cape has provided the first structured space where a range of social partners across the economy, government and civil society are grappling with the meaning of lifelong learning. They are also trying to understand, in preliminary ways, what the relationships are between learning and the economy and society.

ON: The Learning Cape presents the challenge of holding the space to discuss *learning* rather than education and training. In South Africa, formal education is what most people associate with 'learning'. While there has been a long and vibrant history of social movement learning, the learning dimensions of activism within social movements are not readily recognised. Making social learning within informal settings visible is an important dimension of creating the Learning Province. However, it is very difficult to have social learning recognised when there is a strong push (exacerbated by the new competency-based system) for accredited formal education and training, which is associated with work and social mobility.

SW: Within the notion of the Learning Province is a range of theories of development. For example, you can have people highlighting the importance of social capital within a neo-liberal framework, as Mowbray (2004; see also, chapter 4, this volume) pointed out. In this scenario people are being urged to volunteer and to take on more and more community work while the government reduces its public spending in the social sector. There is a new social contract in the 'risk society' where individuals are being told to invest in education throughout their lives. If they fall by the wayside it is their fault.

ON: In some societies, while investment in various aspects of education and training is decreasing, there is inflation in the discourse of lifelong learning (increasing inflation and decreasing investment)! Therefore, does the discourse of the learning society create illusions? Is it not just reinforcing the individual and the market as being in charge of learning and letting governments off the hook? Do we not need more individuals involved, but in a collective framework? Is the 'learning society' just a political slogan?

SW: I think it depends on what notions of development are at play as to what can be achieved by whom. My own view is that participatory development, which involves grassroots organisations, is crucial. The citizens must be 'subjects' not 'objects'. The importance of levels of trust being built through partnerships and networks can be a way of building solidarity and support for poor communities. However, this is not to deny the power struggles and differences that inevitably do exist. There is high unemployment and poverty so the importance of economic growth and development is critical. This goes hand in hand with social development.

ON: Who controls the learning region discourse is important. There will no doubt be ongoing contestations and these are essential if the notions are not going to be left to macro-economists concerned with top-down theories of global development. The discourse of the learning citizen within neo-liberalism is not concerned with the public good – the citizen is the innovative entrepreneur.

SW: The learning region, if it is to become a reality, must be built from the bottom up, cultivating sediments of resilience and ingenuity, which come through supporting learning relationships. Support from the top, in the form of resources, incentives and recognition, is the other side of the coin though.

ON: When we think how difficult it is to solve economic and social problems within the silos of activities, the notion of 'joined-up' approaches seems essential. Also, with the complexities of the world it is easier for most people to relate to their local geographical spaces in which they live. Even though the local spaces are permeated by global influences, their impact can be more easily understood at the local level. This is one of the powerful aspects of the idea of a learning region for me – the connections between the local and the global, and vice versa, through local engagement.

SW: While in our context the odds are stacked against attaining a learning society as imagined through the essential characteristics, don't you think the new forms of organising communities under new circumstances cultivate hope and imagination (Brown, 2002) to perhaps solve old problems in new ways?

ON: Yes, I think so. In thinking about the learning society and learning citizen we need to have a long-term framework and we need to try to undo and avoid opposites. While it is important to recognise the odds stacked against particularly poor people, they are not only victims. The Learning Cape experiences do shine light on a range of creative, imaginative responses which do give hope. I agree with Torres (2003) who argues against 'lifelong learning for the North and basic education for the South' – lifelong learning is critical in the attainment of social justice and economic development. Working with the issues at local level, within a geographical framework, brings the concepts within our grasp.

Notes

[1] Zenobia Africa of ODA drew my attention to these strategies, and as she says, the CDS is long term, it stretches for 20 to 30 years rather than the five years of the Integrated Development Programme. It is a city plan that allows communities, business, learning institutions and government to develop a common set of goals for the city. Their realisation requires not only working out of silo boundaries within the municipality, but exploring wider contacts with other organisations and institutions. For example: The Talent Plan developed by Ottawa to promote learning, education and knowledge industries and to attract people to the city both to learn and to employ skilled inhabitants.

[2] Thanks to Kathy Watters for bringing this example to my attention.

[3] Some of the issues raised were inspired by the public discussion of learning communities held in February 2005 when Chris Duke visited Cape Town. A meeting in Prague of Euronet researchers in October 2004 triggered some others.

Chapter 10

Universities and engagement with cities, regions and local communities

David R. Charles
Centre for Urban and Regional Development Studies,
University of Newcastle, UK

The issue of the engagement of universities with civic society, and inevitably within this with their local communities, is a generic concern internationally. All over the world we observe a huge emphasis being placed on the encouragement of a new set of relationships between universities and their communities. However, whilst we may represent this as a global trend, accelerated perhaps by an exchange of experiences and processes of policy imitation, the form of engagement retains considerable variation. Local contexts vary of course, but national institutional frameworks also differ, and university-community engagement reflects local cultures even whilst translating lessons from elsewhere into local actions.

We tend to reflect these diversities of action either by presenting a limited set of case studies – and it is often interesting which case studies are presented and which are not – or by focusing on small differences between implementations of more standardised interventions. A typical example of the latter is the rapidly growing literature on the commercialisation of university intellectual property. What is perhaps more interesting, however, is the diversity and depth of engagement between university and community in particular places – the formal and the informal, visible and invisible, the exceptional and the mundane. Seeing community engagement as more than widening access and opportunity, innovation and enterprise or simple economic multipliers, requires a concern for the actions of university staff in their institutional and local contexts – a need to join up these actions in a sense of place.

In this chapter we examine the growing interest in universities' engagement with their local regions or communities, and place that in the context of the evolution of the university as an institution. It is argued that regional engagement is not inconsistent with the move towards a university system which is oriented to mass markets and also heavily globalised and competitive. The question of what we mean by the region is, however, not a straightforward one. We examine different national understandings of the region and examine one national typology of forms of regional scales for university engagement. We then look at the range of forms of engagement and specifically address the supposed conflicts between international and regional missions in the contemporary university.

Growing international interest in university regional engagement

University-regional engagement is very topical in Europe at present. In the UK we have seen a plethora of university local economic impact reports, several national reviews of regional engagement (Goddard et al., 1994; Charles and Benneworth, 2001; Campbell et al., 1999; NCIHE, 1997), a government enquiry into university business interactions (Lambert, 2003), the introduction of an annual HE Business Interaction survey (Charles and Conway, 2002), toolkits (Charles and Benneworth, 2002), plus a significant increase in government funding for these activities.

Elsewhere in Europe, against the backdrop of expansion in numbers of institutions (often for regional development purposes) activity has often been more locally initiated, frequently at a city level. City-based public-private partnerships frequently look to universities as key elements in their economic development and urban renaissance initiatives. The lessons of the approaches and mechanisms being used are increasingly subject to international dissemination, both by academic networks such as the Association of European Rectors (CRE) or the OECD's IMHE programme (Goddard and Chatterton, 1999), as well as by the European Union through its structural policies, networking programmes and innovation support. The latter is becoming especially important in the context of the European Research Area concept and the ambitions to raise Europe's R&D spend to 3 per cent of GDP. The European Commission has recently issued a communication intended to start a debate about the role of universities in the 'Europe of Knowledge' (CEC, 2003). In this they specifically examine the balance between the international orientation and the regional role of universities:

There are universities throughout the Union's regions. Their activities often permeate the local economic, social and cultural environment. This helps to make them an instrument of regional development and of strengthening European cohesion. (CEC, 2003, p. 21–2)

Elsewhere, regional engagement has long been a concern in the US as a consequence of state-funded higher education systems (that is, not federal government funded). Aside from the well-rehearsed discussion of spin-offs and clusters, programmes such as the Department of Housing and Urban Development's Community Outreach Partnerships Centers (COPCs) have ensured an engagement with communities as well as with economic development objectives (USDHUD, 2000). Richard Florida's more recent arguments on the creative class (Florida, 2002) also provide a reinforcing argument for the cultural role of universities.

Around the world the story reverberates – incubator policies in Brazil, community engagement in South Africa, the regionalisation of science and innovation policies in Japan, and so on.

There are two main issues here. First is the change in nature of the university itself as an institution, for good or bad, and there is a great debate about this point. Second is the specific spatial scale of engagement and the increasing importance and awareness of the regional or sub-national scale.

The nature of the university

Internationally there is a widespread view that the role of higher education in society has shifted to an increasingly instrumentalist position from a more idealistic one focused on the creation of knowledge (Readings, 1996). This shift is apparent in a number of ways such as through the growing focus on vocational training and the emergence of employability skills within even non-vocational curricula, the growth of contract research and new relations with industrial sponsors, and a perceived erosion of the autonomy and authority of academic governance. Whilst there has been much anguished debate about this within higher education circles (for example, Barnett and Griffin, 1997), these transformations perhaps need to be seen as part of a longer-term historical trajectory. Thus whilst Readings wrote of the ruin of the university as a national institution, an alternative perspective would see the university as an adaptable institution that has always changed in response to, and with implications for, the development of society.

Gerard Delanty (2002) suggests that the university has undergone four revolutions, with current changes being simply the consequence of the last of these, yet building upon earlier changes. It is useful to summarise these revolutions as each reinforces an engagement with society and business, with the erosion of the university as a place apart, and with a particular territorial nature of engagement.

The first revolution was the rise of the Humboldtian university in Germany in the 19th century. The Humboldtian university was a modernising force in society, rational and secular, revolutionary in the link between teaching and research, whereas most universities previously focused on teaching only. Universities also became professionalised with the doctorate being the form of recognition of entry to the profession. Most importantly for our argument though, universities were expected to espouse universal values, and were enrolled by the state to uphold national cultural traditions, underpinning that late nineteenth century obsession with nation-building.

Building on this model, in the late nineteenth century the American university system offered a refinement in the form of the American civic university. Modernisation was taken further here to incorporate in the university mission the role of vocational training, and particularly in the land grant university it became a pragmatic institution, serving the civic community (or its rural equivalent). The focus of teaching moved beyond the professor to the depart-ment, based around disciplines. The key step in engagement was perhaps the idea that universities could provide services to the community, but that these functions were bundled together with other core activities.

In Europe this model was not universally applied, and in many cases the Humboldtian model persisted, sometimes alongside earlier traditions. In the UK the new civic universities initially adopted the American paradigm, but with the steady nationalisation of higher education funding through the twentieth century the civic tradition weakened and a universalist approach prevailed.

The 1960s and massive growth led to the third revolution and the development of the democratic mass university. Social change and increasing participation by a wider social mix of students radicalised the universities, awakening a role in public critique. Knowledge became more democratic, typified by the importance of critical dialogue and the seminar, student participation grew, and there was a loss of autonomy within the university. Engagement in a practical sense was seen as an individual political act for radical academics and students, often against the dominant public authorities, whereas active engagement by the institution itself in partnership with national or local government was disapproved of. E.P. Thompson (1970) wrote a highly critical account of the new Warwick University's attempts to build links with local industry, terming it 'Warwick University Ltd'.

More recently though, the situation has changed again with the weakening of state funding and the rise of competitive threats from the globalisation of the supply of knowledge and of higher education. The certainties of a universalist and modernist agenda have been undermined by postmodernism, and universities have had to become relativistic and multidisciplinary. What Gibbons et al. (1994) have termed 'mode 2 knowledge production' has become more common, although hotly debated and frequently misunderstood and misinterpreted. The reduced state contribution per student and the need to find alternative sources of funds has inspired forms of academic capitalism and the related idea of the triple helix of government, higher education and business entwined and mutually engaged (Etzkowitz, 2004), stimulating innovation in managerial structures, and the importation of private sector models and mores into the academy.

The consequent concern about the future of the university, especially from traditionalists, has been termed by some 'the end of knowledge' and the decline of the university of culture. Certainly the idea of the national liberal university is in crisis, but the crisis is perhaps overstated, as the model of the university mutates and adapts to changed conditions.

The scale of investment in the expansion of higher education and the emergence of massification were inevitably going to change the nature of the sector. Expansion to a current level of 30–40 per cent of school leavers, in addition to increased numbers of mature students, would inevitably have a dramatic effect on the character of universities. The wider social mix and aspirations of students were coupled with a demand from government that much university capacity should be devoted to preparing students for work. With small numbers in higher education, a tradition of residential study away from home could be maintained, and indeed this was still apparent in the debates about the location of new universities in the UK in the Robbins expansion of the 1960s (Committee on Higher Education, 1963). However, with mass higher education, and the retreat from student grants, home-based provision has become much more important and universities are now much more widely distributed in most countries. Although a more traditional form of higher education remains in certain institutions, the consequence is a much more diverse and locally focused sector than previously, within which community and employer relevance is inevitable.

The demand for a more massive higher education sector parallels a wider set of changes in society and the economy, commonly referred to as the emergence of a knowledge-based economy, or sometimes described as a learning economy (Lundvall and Borrás, 1997). The transformation of workplaces and the relative growth of knowledge-based office occupations is manifested through demand for greater numbers of graduates.

Additionally the forms of knowledge needed are continuously shifting away from traditional disciplinary lines to new problem-focused themes (Gibbons et al., 1994). Hence within research collaboration and mainstream training and education there has been a growth in new combinations of expertise, and new centres and departments that map into the needs of employers.

What do we mean by region and community?

The problem of defining a university's local community is both philosophical as well as methodological. Universities are not discrete entities separate from, but interacting with, some kind of spatially defined market. Rather, the university is embedded in many different types of 'community': some local, some global, some overlapping and interacting, some barely recognising each other. In this sense the university is an essential part of local, national and global society, and forms part of how we define our society.

One of the most fascinating aspects of the university-community dialogue between Europe and Australia is the different conceptualisation of the idea of the region, and the nature of the territorial development problem. I was puzzled when I first visited Australia by some of the statements I heard about the nature of regions, and particularly the idea that 'regional universities' were essentially a group of universities based outside of the metropolitan centres. It became clear that the word was being used in a different sense and it is revealing to expand on this.

In Europe there is a shared understanding of regional as sub-national units of territorial analysis or governance. Countries (or indeed Europe itself – the

'Europe of the regions') are divided into regions for the purpose of policy delivery and governance. All parts of a national territory are divided into regions, often reflecting historical cultural identities, sometimes recently imposed bureaucratic mechanisms, but usually some form of service area focused on a city. European regions are mainly city-regions – cities with a surrounding hinterland, the few exceptions being diffuse peripheral areas on the northern margins. What is clear though is that the idea of a large metropolitan area as a region is probably the rule rather than the exception. Unlike Australia, there is no sense of regions as primarily non-metropolitan areas.

This difference in conceptualising the region rests on two main issues. First, the distances between major cities in Europe are such that most of the non-urban areas are within the daily urban system of the big cities – rural hinterlands are connected to the cities in a much more immediate and direct way than is possible for many Australian 'regions'. The second issue is that there is not the same geography of economic disparity between city and rural area in Europe and Australia. Many of the European cities have extreme development needs and have concentrations of the most economically disad-vantaged communities, often alongside great wealth, whilst there are both rich rural areas as well as impoverished remote regions. The map of disparity in Europe is an extremely complex mosaic requiring a rich mix of urban and rural development policies, with regional policies being concerned with the balances between regions, as well as developing appropriate internal regional spatial development strategies. The levels of policy themselves are highly complex – European cohesion policies which address high level disparities, as well as supporting bottom-up capacity-building in locally disadvantaged areas; national regional redistributive policies; and policies focused on urban as well as rural development implemented by national, regional and local government.

For an institution such as the university there is a highly complex regional policy environment – sometimes managed by spatial or territorial policies and sometimes more sectorally-focused. Universities need to carefully pick their way through the maze of policies and the complex relationships they may have with the territorial agencies around them. Returning to the issue of the small size of many European regions, there may be considerable disjuncture between the service territories of universities and the regional boundaries defined by government, with important consequences if the government seeks to use the regions to influence university engagement.

When it comes to how universities perceive the idea of their own regions, there are four aspects of their definitions of a local community which can be developed with examples drawn from the UK (Goddard et al., 1994):

- the relationship between an institution and its physical surroundings as influenced by historical and institutional context;
- the different scales at which attributes or impacts of the university should be measured or assessed;
- the different geographic scale or territory over which the university provides different types of 'local' service;
- the perceptions held by the institution and its management of the local community which is identified in institutional plans and through related activities.

Historical and cultural contexts

Different types of institutions can be used to illustrate the effect of their historical development upon the external (and perhaps internal) perception of their locality. Five broad groups of examples of university institution in the UK can be used to illustrate the heterogeneity of circumstances, although we recognise that this is not a typology that satisfactorily encompasses all institutions, or indeed necessarily translates into other countries.

First we can begin with the historical university town (Oxford, Cambridge, St Andrews, for example). These towns and universities present an interesting paradox in terms of local identity and community. In all four cases the physical form and function of the city centre has been dominated by the buildings of the university. Such towns developed around the colleges; the image and perception of the place therefore becomes synonymous with the university, yet these institutions are explicitly international in orientation, and tensions exist between local people and a detached, and in some senses walled-off, enclave or 'ivory tower'.

We can counter this with examples, mainly of former polytechnics, emerging from a municipal college background where the place may not be closely identified with higher education, but where the university identifies closely with its town. In other words the sense of community is a clearly articulated mission to serve the town in which the institution is based and where control formerly resided (Coventry, Sunderland, Derby, for example).

Between these two distinct groups lie the metropolitan 'red brick', or 'civic' universities. Although often established with the support of urban municipalities, the 'civic' universities tend to be identified most clearly as regional institutions. Even in their early years, as the only universities within particular regions, the 'civic' universities tended to attract and cultivate wider interests than those of the city cores. In Newcastle, for example, the historic industrial ties have been with the Tyneside conurbation; links are also strong with the aristocratic and agricultural interests of rural Northumberland; whilst in terms of health care the university is a focus for training and, through the teaching hospitals, specialised health care for the whole region.

In contrast to the 'civic' universities with their urban core locations but regional vision, many of the Robbins period campus universities remain somewhat detached from their localities. Out-of-town campuses and an absence of strong 'rooting' faculties, such as medicine, combined with their small scale has tended to limit the local impact of such institutions, which often feel the need to strive to develop a community role.

Finally a special form of place-traversing institution is emerging, with some form of regional identity mobilised through decentralised campuses. An early example of this was the University of Ulster, with its multiple sites in non-urban locations. Anglia is another example of a regional multi-site institution. As some former city-council controlled universities reposition themselves as regional, and potentially networked, institutions, so the identification with a single town or city becomes subsumed in a new regional identity.

Impact assessment scales
Defining what constitutes a local community represents a major challenge for any analysis of the economic impact of a university. In only a few instances will the local administrative area (district or county) constitute a meaningful entity for economic analysis. University employees will not necessarily live and work within this administrative area or spend the bulk of their income within it. Some universities are part of large and complex metropolitan systems where there is a greater likelihood of the expenditure being contained within the city region, while others are smaller towns with more limited services.

However, whilst employment-based impacts need to be assessed at the labour market scale, expenditure on goods and services may be more sensibly assessed at a different scale. Thus where a university is in a small labour market but adjacent to a major urban centre, expenditure leakage to the major city will be high. In this case it may be more sensible to consider the larger functional regions, based on the conurbations, in which these smaller towns are enfolded.

In general however the definition of the area will depend on the rationale of the investigation, on whether a particular territorially-defined body (local authority or regional organisation) is sponsoring or to be influenced by any study, or on the university's own definition of its community. The wider the area defined, the greater the absolute impact as leakage is reduced, but the less significant the scale relative to total economic activity.

Service territories

Whilst we can define the local labour market area as the appropriate scale for assessing employment effects, it must be recognised that there are different geographic scales or territories over which the university provides different types of 'local' services. Different services have different natural catchment areas, some highly local and others more extensive, depending on the degree of specialisation or exclusivity of the service and the distance customers are prepared to travel to make use of it. So whilst a university sports facility will usually have a very localised demand, technology transfer services may be regional or even international in scope.

So when discussing the concept of a local community, it is important to bear in mind that for different individuals within the institution, their 'local' community may be very different in scale. It is also important to remember that only some universities operate particular services that have a genuine regional role, such as medical schools.

Institutional plans

Finally, any study of the university and its communities must take account of the university's perception of what constitutes the local community and over what scale its institutional plan is active. University institutional plans often refer to specific local communities. In the case of old universities these may be laid down in the statutes. For example the statutes of the University of Southampton refer to the five counties of Dorset, Hampshire, Isle of Wight, West Sussex and Wiltshire. Several of the new universities were created as multi-site institutions and the distribution of these sites has determined their regions.

Other universities are staking out their regional turf through the creation of new sites or establishing franchise arrangements with further and higher education colleges and, by implication, defining their own catchment areas.

Many universities also have a two-tier definition of their localities. For example, Warwick identifies the local area as embracing Coventry,

Warwick and Solihull, and its region as comprising the West Midlands. Such distinctions may map onto the tiered structure of local government from districts and counties through to the standard regions defined by central government.

Multiple geometries

What should be clear from the above is that universities do not just have one region but many, overlapping and nested, used at different times and for different purposes according to historical contingency and evolving patterns of interaction. These different scales and interactions make the development of strategy complex, and that is without consideration of national and international relationships; but it is essential in complex organisations such as universities to recognise the multi-stranded and multiple level nature of external interactions. These interactions are also differentiated by theme, and, in addition, we need to consider the types of projects and actions that will have a particular regional dimension and contribute in developmental terms to the university's region.

Conceptualising the regional mission

In recent years the notion of regional development has changed from a view of targeted policies to redress the problems of uneven growth in areas that are lagging, to a more positive understanding of the need for all regions to develop the ability to enhance or simply maintain their economic performance and social cohesion through policies that are sensitive to different asset bases and historic trajectories. Often this is described using the terminology of regional competition. Places can be said to compete in the sense that they engage in rivalry in creating or attracting activities that generate wealth for their citizens. This ability to provide the wherewithal to be successful in these terms is commonly described by the concept of competitiveness.

Territorial/place competitiveness can therefore be assumed to be the ability of places to add value to the activity of business through the interaction of a set of framework conditions (such as wage costs, the quality of labour, infrastructure endowment, and so on), with a set of inter-business and local institutional relations, in such a way that business can become more successful against international competition. But, in addition, in order to be reproducible in the longer term, the benefits of wealth generation must be redistributed within the region to enhance social equity and quality of life without compromising sustainability.

More precisely, regional competitiveness can be defined as *the ability of the constituent members of a region to take action to ensure that business based within that region is selling greater levels of value added against international competition, sustained by the assets and institutions of the region, thereby contributing to rising GDP and a broad distribution of wealth across the population, yielding a high standard of living, and a virtuous cycle of learning effects.*

We therefore need to look beyond business success to include also the means of maintaining social cohesion and the quality of life in successful regions. If this is considered as a set of broad processes, then seven main groups of processes can be identified and incorporated into a simple model:

- *Regional framework conditions*: the regional infrastructure, regulatory frameworks and underlying quality of environment and lifestyles.
- *Human capital development*: the development of human capital through education and training.
- *Business development*: the creation and attraction of new firms within the region, as well as the development of new products, processes and markets.
- *Interactive learning and social capital development*: co-operation between firms and other institutions to generate technological, commercial and social benefits as well as developing new skills in individuals.
- *Redistribution*: ensuring that the benefits of enhanced business competitiveness are widely shared within the community and that the health and welfare of the population is maximised.
- *Regional cultural development*: the creation, enhancement and reproduction of regional cultures, underpinning the other processes above, and interpreting culture both as activities that enrich the quality of life but also as patterns of social conventions, norms and values that constitute regional identities.
- *Sustainability*: long-term regional development must be underpinned by processes seeking to improve the prospects for sustainability, even though some of these objectives may appear to conflict with business development objectives.

If these processes underpin regional or place competitiveness then how do the activities of universities in supporting that ambition map into these processes? Each of the processes above can be recast in terms of the potential university contribution to varying degrees.

Regional framework conditions are in some senses the most difficult aspects of a region for a university to affect, although as large employers and businesses, universities have the ability to lobby local infrastructure providers, or in some cases take on infrastructure provision themselves. They affect external perception of regional attractiveness through their effects on talent attraction, and through their research they can influence policies that underpin the wider economic environment. A strategic awareness of the role of the university in its local environment is central to its ability to influence this aspect of the region, as is the existence of a consensus with other key local factors as to the direction of this influence.

The human capital role of a university is much clearer and relates centrally to the teaching and learning role. However, a university can still have a limited regional impact on the human capital of a region if students are not retained in the region or if no attempt is made to raise the skills of people based in the region. Significant impact will depend on clearly articulated paths for local students to aspire to, and participate in, higher education; on some orientation of the degree programmes and their mode of delivery to regional needs; and on attempts to assist the retention of students within the region. This is not to say that the university should seek to encourage students to stay in the region against their best interests, but working with local employers to identify and develop good graduate opportunities and actively promote them to students may be regarded as good practice.

Business development is also commonly regarded as central to the regional mission of the university. Whilst at the core this is focused on innovation and new business ventures, it is by no means restricted to this. The commercialisation of university expertise is a recurrent preoccupation at present and there are many mechanisms developed to support this, but this should include support for enterprise amongst graduates and forms of knowledge transfer embodying people through various forms of placement. In addition, the expertise transferred need not be technical but could include language and cultural awareness for firms exporting into new markets, or wider business skills. The university can also be used to help attract new businesses into the region through a combination of its research expertise, the promise of a flow of graduates and the effect on the general attractiveness of the region.

Interactive learning and social capital formation is separated out from human capital formation to reinforce the distinction between the normal educational process, which involves imparting students with 'know why' and 'know what' forms of knowledge, and a wider concept of learning which includes 'know how' and 'know who' (Lundvall and Johnson, 1994). At a regional level we are also concerned with the learning that takes place across different policy communities, through socialised forms of learning in what we might term communities of practice. Universities can be central players in these processes through the participation of staff in various boards, committees and working groups, and through the sharing of knowledge in different fora. Another term for this could be civic responsibility, and this relates to the notion that academic tenure and freedom is not a right, but a responsibility to speak up without fear of political or employer pressure (McDowell, 2001).

In our model of regional development we noted the importance of redistribution to ensure that competitiveness is not undermined by the polarisation of society. Again, this is perhaps more a national economic agenda than one for the universities, but universities can have an effect both through their own access policies – and the consequences for social mobility – as well as through interventions aimed at encouraging inclusiveness and supporting the most vulnerable groups in society. This could include working with disadvantaged communities to build capabilities, or the delivery of services direct to children with disadvantaged backgrounds or to other groups which are entitled to public support. A particular dimension of this in some countries is voluntary community activity by students (HEFCE, 2004).

Culture is increasingly seen as a key element in regional development, an economic sector in its own right; an important element of quality of life and attractiveness to talented people; and an element of building social cohesion. Universities have a strong role to play in the development of culture in a region through the provision of cultural facilities, the activities of their students, the creation of a base of demand for additional cultural facilities and their project management roles. The nature of the cultural role will vary according to the kind of location – between a metropolitan core and a small town location for example – and there are national variations in the recognition of the cultural role, but it is an element of the mission that seems to be growing in significance.

The final element in this overview is the sustainability agenda and the role that universities can play, both through their own responsible use of resources, as well as through their demonstration and educational contributions to sustainability policies. As large centres of employment and study, universities can have quite significant local environmental impacts, yet they have the knowledge base to develop workable solutions not only to their own impacts but also to those of other organisations – indeed many provide environmental consulting to businesses or public authorities – and play a key role in local sustainability fora.

These different strands of activity add up to have positive effects on the local region, but we need to ask if they simply make a marginal difference or whether they can be strategically directed as part of a comprehensive regional mission. What this points towards is the need for an integrated approach, within which there is a consensus between regional stakeholders in terms of addressing regional needs. In such a system, links are forged between functionally-divided areas within the university and the region, allowing multiple needs to be addressed. Within the university, the challenge then is to link all areas of activity encompassing the teaching, research and community service roles by internal mechanisms (such as funding, staff development, incentives and rewards, and communication). Within the region the challenge is to engage the university with all facets of the development process, embracing, for example, skills, technological development, cultural awareness, community regeneration and environmental protection, in a region/university value-added management process.

Acknowledgement

This paper builds on work over many years and with many colleagues and research partners. I particularly want to thank John Goddard, Cheryl Conway and Paul Benneworth, along with the partners in the UNIREG project, which I coordinated and which was funded by the EU 4th Framework Programme (1999–2000). I also want to acknowledge that specific parts of this chapter draw on material developed for the 'Universities and Communities' project for the then CVCP (now Universities UK), and the Regional Mission project for HEFCE and Universities UK.

Chapter 11
Sustainable Development

Sara Parkin* and Kate Sankey**

*Co-founder and Programme Director, Forum for the Future, London, UK; **Deputy Director, Division of Academic Innovation and Continuing Education, Institute of Education, University of Stirling, Scotland, UK.

Sustainable development is perhaps the single most fundamental policy area facing the world in the twenty-first century. As a topic for taking seriously, it is certainly hot, perhaps too hot to handle.

This chapter summarises a longer study by Sara Parkin published as a Pascal Hot Topic. The original paper presents a very full thesis arguing the necessity to take a radically new way of approaching sustainable development as a key policy area. This chapter sets out the bones of the argument for consideration of a conceptual framework that is holistic, integrated and systemic, intellectually robust but crucially eminently understandable. As a way of making critical survival decisions it must also be a practical tool for people to engage and contribute at all levels.

The term 'sustainable capitalism' is developed from a consideration of the intellectual legacy inherited from the European Enlightenment and the Industrial Revolution. This is presented as a single, portable, easy-to-use and conceptually robust way to think about what the key sustainability questions might be in the first place. It explores an intellectual framework to help make sense of the world, whether those questions are posed at the level of the earth's ecological systems, a country, a local authority, a business, a university, a corner shop or a household.

The overall goal is to seek a path for human progress, and to secure a future that is more mind and soul nourishing than growing gross domestic product (GDP) year on year.

Issues relating to sustainable development are powerfully presented by charities and voluntary organisations that have worked in various specialist fields for decades. Organisations like WWF, Amnesty International, Save the Children and Church Action on Poverty highlight the results of unsustainable development, be they manifest in human or environmental degradation (see, for example, Christie and Warburton, 2001). Other evidence has been presented by governmental bodies and prestigious institutes that range from the UN Panel on Climate Change, to the House of Lords Select Committees, to the American Academy of Science, to the Meteorological Office. With varying degrees of scientific precision, they all try to bring together current knowledge of a global picture that is clear enough to guide policy at all levels. The emphasis on the individual and local community responsibility within a policy framework that focuses on partnership-working, further highlights the value for sustainable development to feature as an underlying concept on the place management, social capital and learning region agendas.

This is a particularly important time for all as the UK government seeks to gather support for the UK-shared framework for sustainable development, *One Future – Different Paths* (Defra, 2005a) and in England the published strategy *Securing the Future* (Defra, 2005b). It is recognised that implementation on the ground for such a framework will depend on building local capacity and social capital. The Egan Report on delivering skills for sustainable communities (ODPM, 2004a) highlights the need for 'understanding sustainable development' and 'understanding the economics of development and the processes of local democracy'. This report is part of an ongoing commitment of the Office of the Deputy Prime Minister (ODPM, 2003). A summit was held in February 2005 (ODPM, 2005) demonstrating the holistic approach to sustainable development required. Sustainable communities 'meet the diverse needs of existing and future residents, are sensitive to the environment, and contribute to a high quality of life'.

Furthermore, this is a time when global warming and global poverty are now considered together, and the power of people as individuals, families, communities and institutions is being realised through the growing engagement and a willingness to seek solutions. Internationally the debate rages and global alliances stand and fall as the world tackles these issues.

But there is another dimension to the story of human progress, life and the universe. Hopefulness and happiness as an overall purpose for the human species should be reclaimed by policy makers, where success is far more than any value-free, free-market economic system measured in production and consumption. Unfortunately, in the European Enlightenment's struggle taking place in the eighteenth century (to secularise morality in order to make Man's rationality, rather than that of the Church, the legitimate decision-making system for political and social leaders), finer sensibilities – including morality and happiness – lost out. The intellectual and political rush to find a logical system that could pursue the greatest happiness of the greatest number left by the wayside the various higher values and virtues that had acted as either guide or governor (and which largely predate the birth of modern religions) on human behaviour.

The vision of sustainable development encompasses all aspects of human/ environment interactions and interdependence. Thus well-being and 'happiness' can become the legitimate goal of the collective as well as of individual endeavour (see, for example, Easterlin, 2001; Frey and Stutzer, 2002).

There are warning signs – for example in the light of the apparent victory of the 'Moral Majority' in the November 2004 US Presidential elections, some may feel that morality is right back up there as an equal partner with economics – and that, therefore, the ultimately unsuccessful Enlightenment project of uniting economic and moral objectives in the hands of rational people instead of church dogma is back on track. But it would be wrong to assume this to be the case. Defending the role of reason and argument in ethics, Princeton philosopher Peter Singer has carried out a clinical dissection of the moral philosophy of George Bush, and failed to find a consistent definition of right and wrong or good and evil in the President's utterances and actions, nor a consistency of either with human rights, Utilitarianism, or even Christianity. Moreover, Singer could not identify a consistency in the way Bush uses his famous instinct, what he calls his 'gut feeling'. This seems to imply that the President of the Earth's only super-state operates with no personal set of guiding or governing values of any kind (Singer, 2004). How did it get lost – a neglected strand of thinking from the European Enlightenment?

There is one strand that did not resonate down the centuries, unlike the voices of the founder of classical economics Adam Smith and his intellectual progeny, but one which probably holds the best chance of reuniting the disparate economic, social and philosophical ambitions of our species around a common, and higher, purpose. It came from James Hutton, born in 1723 (the same year as Adam Smith), who in 1795 published to great acclaim a geological version of Smith's massively influential *Wealth of Nations*. In *Theory of the Earth*, Hutton observed that 'this world has neither beginning nor an end', and described the continual renewal cycles of the natural world as having one purpose – that of life itself. 'We are thus led to see a circulation in the matter of this globe, and a system of beautiful economy in the works of nature' (Hutton, 1795).

There is real evidence that the currency of a responsible approach to ethics and values is indeed gaining value. Sceptical though we should be, the rush of businesses to be seen as virtuous and ethical through their corporate social responsibility (CSR) activities is evidence that they recognise that their customers care more about these things than they did in the past.

Following the story from beginning to end, this chapter offers a guide for a twenty-first century 'survival trail'. How will we know whether we are on the right route? Aldo Leopold provides a signpost: 'A thing is right when it tends to preserve the integrity, stability and beauty of the biotic community. It is wrong when it tends otherwise' (Leopold, 1949).

Lester Milbrath signals the essential element of understanding and thinking that must accompany us on the survival trail, 'it is absolutely essential to change the way we think. All other attempts at change will fail if we do not transform our thinking...A proper understanding of the way the world works requires people to think systemically, holistically, integratively, and in a futures mode' (Milbrath, 1996).

By implication, Leopold and Milbrath point to the existence of fundamental laws of the human/earth co-evolution partnership. This is a world where ignorance or flagrant breaking of these laws has consequences.

Before exploring how we might combine James Hutton's theory of the world with that of Adam Smith in order to craft a new theory for taking our species into a successful twenty-first century and beyond, we must examine some of the laws that should, and must, guide and govern how our species progresses forward in time. In reality they are all part and parcel of the same basic law of the Earth – that everything is connected. Everything on Earth is in a special relationship, or as James Lovelock, the chemist who brought James Hutton's theory of the Earth as one system up to date for the twentieth century would say: all aspects of the atmospheric gases and surface rocks and water are regulated by the growth, death, metabolism and other activities of living organisms (Lovelock, 1979). Most recently, climate scientists in the largest, most rigorously reviewed research project of all time have added even more evidence of the Earth as one system as they discover more about the intimate relationships between clouds, shrinking ice coverage, ocean currents, micro-organisms and so on.

A starting point, therefore, for the learning journey is to grasp the significance of the fundamentals. It is useful to look at six elements governing life: *ecology, evolution, biology, physics, spirituality* and the *human species*.

The challenge is to see ourselves as part of a system, able to alter the course and speed of evolution, and too often not understanding the most basic and obvious interdependence of the life-support systems. For example, by ignoring the ecological, evolutionary, biological and physical systems derived from complex, interconnected systems of water, air, soil and nutrition and their products, we are mindlessly creating waste products and pollution. The idea of a hierarchical Chain of Being with the human species at the top is a nonsense derived from otherwise helpful methods of classifying living organisms.

Over the past twenty years or so, Fritjof Capra (1982, 1996) has deepened and broadened our capacity to see how the principles of ecological relationships – the systems that operate at all levels – can guide us not only in our relationship with 'others' in the living world, but within our own minds and social systems. Resilience in a biological system, Capra explains, is created by dense and systemic networking of living systems at different levels: chemical interactions; molecular and cellular organisation; species symbiosis; global ecosystems. The same resilience can be brought into the human endeavour by using the same networking principles. *Vernetztes Denken*, or network thinking, for example, regularly exposes the errors of understanding (and therefore failure to take wise decisions) that arise from isolating 'bits' of what is actually part of one system. So what of the spirit? Fritjof Capra points out that the word for *soul* and for *spirit* means *breath* in many different languages. Thinking about the connection between the breath of our inner life and that of our outer one may not work for everyone, but most people are searching for a deeper meaning for life than a purely materialist one and it doesn't take much for them to connect their own physical and mental well-being with that of the environment.

The final section of Tim Jackson's book *Material Concerns* points out that, by accepting material definitions of wealth, society has:

> accepted a kind of poisoned chalice. Offering sanctity of choice,
> fulfilment of our desires, and the greater good of fellow human
> beings, has delivered environmental destruction, economic

> instability and new alarming kinds of poverty: poverty of identity,
> poverty of community, and poverty of spirit. (Jackson, 1996)

It is this impoverishment – over and above material poverty – that creates the sort of black hole of the soul that too easily sucks in extremist and simplistic representations of any spiritual certainty whether it is touted by high priests of Anglicanism, Islam, the New Age or nihilism.

There remains therefore a question as to whether the disastrous effects of our species acting in a selfish way are actually inevitable, given that we operate within cultures which reward competitive and individualistic behaviour. The consequences of breaking laws are predicable – you get caught and have to pay the consequences. The writing is on the wall – population growth, over-loading and unfair appropriation of the earth's life support systems, exploitation of the earth's natural capital, climate change and so forth, are all indicators of the lack of sustainability of our current economic systems.

However, this chapter seeks not to frame the crisis as total doom and gloom but to present a way out, by building a new logic to develop a personal and societal intellectual framework. It is a crisis of implementation requiring a behavioural change. This new logic builds on the concept of sustainable development as the process whereby, over time, we achieve sustainability. There are rumoured to be over 200 definitions of *sustainable development*; it has become fashionable nowadays to say that it actually defies definition as it is too complex. This is not strictly true. It is not so much the definition that is difficult, but making it happen in practice. No end of changing the language can avoid the fact that, in the end, you have to do it.

Perhaps the best known definition is the one coined in the 1987 Brundtland Report: 'Humanity has the ability to make development sustainable – to ensure that it meets the need of the present without compromising the ability of future generations to meet their own needs' (World Commission on Environment and Development, 1987).

Capturing this integrated objective and building on what we now know about the process and the goal, the 2005 UK Sustainable Development Strategy brings the definition into the twenty-first century:

> The goal of sustainable development is to enable all people throughout the world to satisfy their basic needs and enjoy a better quality of life, without compromising the quality of life of future generations. For the UK government and the Devolved

Administrations, that goal will be pursued in an integrated way through a sustainable, innovative and productive economy that delivers high levels of employment; and a just society that promotes social inclusion, sustainable communities and personal wellbeing. This will be done in ways that protect and enhance the physical and natural environment, and use resources and energy as efficiently as possible. (Defra, 2005b)

Comprehending that sustainable development is about progressing economic, social and environmental goals simultaneously is gaining currency. Businesses and others often talk about sustainability as a 'triple bottom line', or as a Venn diagram of overlapping circles. But while such characterisations are really helpful in clarifying the nature of the challenge of sustainable development, they still don't get us very much further in understanding the challenge in a practical sense. At present it is the economy that drives how we must do things as a society (compete not collaborate, for example) and which currently thrives best where it can substitute off-balance-sheet environmental degradation for on-balance-sheet costs. These are the inevitable consequences of marginalising the role of the scientific laws of the Earth. These laws, tested by evolution over aeons, have been totally marginalised in the model for economic success that we currently use as a proxy for success of the whole human endeavour.

The true picture and real bottom line is the environment. It sets the limits that everything else must respect. Next in the hierarchy is society. It is we human beings who set the parameters – the goals – and the ethics and values that will govern and guide achieving those goals for our development. There is a range of mechanisms for making those decisions – some individual, some collective – as a family, at work, as an electorate. We have the power to choose to do things differently. And finally, nested within society is the economy. Ideally it should be structured in a way that enables society to meet its objectives, within its ethical framework, and obviously respecting environmental limits.

The man who gave the model based on the economy and capitalism a philosophy was Adam Smith who, in 1776, published *The Wealth of Nations* (Smith, 1776) in which he formulated his minute observations of British society into an overarching model of 'the market'. Writing 230 years ago, Smith saw the market harnessing individual selfishness to provide a flow of benefits to all. He had unreserved confidence that it would lead in the direction 'which is most agreeable to the interest of the whole society'. So while Adam

Smith did see that his theory of the self-regulating marketplace needed people and the environment to meet its demands rather than the other way round – 'the demand for men, like the demand for any other commodity, necessarily regulates the production of men' (Heilbroner, 1983, p. 50) – it is unlikely that James Hutton saw in his theory of life on Earth as one continuous bio-chemical market-place a model that could challenge that of his contemporary.

Although he was not the first to comment on the market, Smith was the first to formulate its workings in a wide and systematic fashion. Today's ferment of observation and critique of social history and relations (including market economics and capitalism) is a continuation of the debate that Smith started. Because the world is now a very different place, the search for a new logical framework to make sense of what is happening and to bring order and meaning is throwing up new theories. This is not least because Adam Smith did not forecast the first industrial revolution, which was underway before he published *The Wealth of Nations*. His edict to 'let good emerge as the by-product of selfishness' has not delivered automatically, as he believed it would. As a more recent commentator, Francis Fukuyama, put it, 'the tendency of contemporary liberal democracies to fall prey to excessive individualism is perhaps their greatest long term vulnerability' (Fukuyama, 1999).

The challenge, remember, is to achieve economic, social and environmental goals together, and to do so despite the fact that they are persistently dis-aggregated into different government departments, school subjects, university disciplines and different pages of the newspaper. This makes thinking about sustainable development, never mind doing it, extremely difficult. Our social and economic world has been actively prevented from evolving in the same way that the biochemical world does. We have historically co-evolved with other species – as a whole, and at the same time – but at least our minds evolved with the capacity to handle complexity and subtlety, not least in our social relations. So there seems to be no reason why our collective minds can't create a new, Hutton-inspired and integrated way of thinking about our place in the world, and how we might handle our relationship with it better.

This is where the idea of sustainable capitalism comes in. The starting point is to consider the definition of capital. The meaning of the word in accepted commercial terms covers any stock of assets – financial or physical – capable of generating income. Yet when it comes to deciding what assets are to be included, there are many opinions. This is helpful because the most logical route to achieving sustainable development would seem to be to shift – or rather extend – the definition of capital. A question can be posed: just what are the assets (or resources) available to us as we try to live within the laws of the Earth, and as happily as possible with each other? Described in some detail by Paul Ekins (Ekins et al., 1992) the 'four capital model' has been developed by, amongst others, the World Bank (Serageldin and Steer, 1994) and Forum for the Future.

Five categories of capital assets – natural, human, social, manufactured, financial – have been identified. Table 11.1 explains in more detail what is represented by each stock of assets. The point is that if investment in each of the assets is sufficient to maintain and enhance *all* of the capital stocks at the same time, then a flow of benefits can be expected. In theory at least, that flow of benefits will constitute a path for the human endeavour that could be described as sustainable (that is, capable of continuing into the long-term future). In practice, the causal link between benefit flow and capital stock may be less than absolutely certain, but it will certainly be good enough to take us off an unsustainable trajectory and in a new direction towards a sustainable way of life.

It may seem historically arrogant to say that just as Adam Smith grew his unifying and clarifying theories from observation, so too grows the theory of the five capitals. In reality, however, we are only knitting back together theories about the evolution of the Earth and about the evolution of society that should never have been separated in the first place. Indeed, in many cultures the notion of the environment and society as indivisible still endures. It is only the children of the European Enlightenment who ended up developing the one hypothesis (Smith's) to the exclusion of others (Hutton's).

Table 11.1 Sustainable capitalism: the five capitals

Financial Capital is viewed by many as different from the other four capitals in that it has, strictly speaking, no intrinsic value; whether in shares, bonds or banknotes, its value is purely representative of natural, human, social or manufactured capital. Financial capital is nevertheless very important as it reflects the productive power of the other types of capital and enables them to be owned or traded. Some would argue that a society's 'trust' in financial capital as a means of exchange is an important element of social capital.

Manufactured Capital comprises all human fabricated 'infrastructure' that is already in existence. The tools, machines, roads, buildings in which we live and work, and so on. It does not include the goods and services that are produced by them. In some cases manufactured capital may be viewed as a source of materials (building waste used as aggregate for road building or repair, for example).

Social Capital is all the different cooperative systems and organisational frameworks people use to live and work together, such as families, communities, governments, businesses, schools, trade unions and voluntary groups. Although they involve different types of relationships and organisation they are all structures or institutions that add value to human capital, and tend to be successful in doing so if based on mutual trust and shared purpose (Putnam, 2000). Again, the importance of social capital is only recently being recognised, unfortunately through the increasingly visible negative effects when it is eroded.

Human Capital consists of the health, knowledge, skills, motivation and spiritual ease of people, that is, all the things that enable people to feel good about themselves, each other, participating in society and contributing productively towards its well-being (wealth). Recently recognised as providing a high return on investment, especially in developing societies where investment in human resources is viewed as possibly the most essential ingredient of development strategies (UNDP, 1999) but also in the highly industrialised world (Edvinsson and Malone, 1997).

Natural Capital (also referred to as environmental or ecological capital) represents the stock of environmentally provided assets and falls into two categories:

Resources, some of which are renewable (trees, vegetation, fish, water), and others non-renewable (fossil fuels, minerals). In some places ostensibly renewable resources (like fertile soil) have become non-renewable (desert).

Services, such as climate regulation or the powerful waste processing cycles that breakdown, absorb, and recycle emissions and waste from all species.

Based on Parkin, 2000a, 2000b.

Indeed, a reflection on the laws of the Earth reveals that in reality, there are only two sources of wealth and well-being: that which flows from the resources and services provided by the Earth (natural capital), and that which flows from our own hands, brains and spirits (human capital). Everything else derives from these two primary sources. As one of the early ecological economists was fond of pointing out, 'in the beginning Man [sic] lay naked on the grass. The mistake we made was to account for everything he created around him (clothes, shelter etc) financially instead of biologically' (Georgescu-Roegen, 1971). Go a bit further, and given that the human species is a miraculous assemblage of basic natural elements in continual exchange with the elements around us, we could say that human capital is in fact a subset of nature – a true if sobering thought that confirms the overriding importance of achieving environmental sustainability.

Forum for the Future and others are already using the five capital model to provide an adaptable but rigorous sustainability framework in which to design or audit ideas, decisions and initiatives in a way that ensures that they are more likely to favour sustainable development than to undermine it. These others include, for example, the Department for International Development, Wessex Water, Co-operative Bank and Interface, a large carpet company.

Interestingly, when people set about describing what benefits they feel would flow from suitably healthy stocks of the capital assets, the result is, if not a modern-day version of Arcadia, then certainly close to the aspirations of most people – for themselves and their families. Table 11.2 gives some examples.

Table 11.2 Sustainable capitalism: stocks and flows of five capital assets

Financial	STOCK: money, stocks, bonds
	FLOW: *means of valuing, owning, exchanging other four*
Manufactured	STOCK: tools, infrastructure, buildings
	FLOW *Places to live, work, play; access to them*
Social	STOCK: governance systems, communities, families
	FLOW: *security, justice, social inclusion*
Human	STOCK: health, knowledge, motivation, spiritual ease
	FLOW: *energy, work, creativity, love, happiness*
Natural	STOCK: land, sea, air, rivers, ecological systems
	FLOW: *biodiversity, energy, food, water, climate, waste disposal*

This way of looking at definitions of sustainability and of expanding our idea of what constitutes capital assets available to us as a species as we contemplate progress in the twenty-first century, does provide us with a robust and logical intellectual framework. Within this we can work out what to do in a way that is more likely to contribute to sustainable development (that is, make a positive contribution to maintaining or enhancing all five capitals together).

A practical example might be a new social housing project. It may surpass the highest energy efficiency standards, helping to maintain natural capital, and may have delivered significant improvement in the stock of human and social capital through better health and reduced vandalism. But if it was built on part of a park rather than on a brownfield site, thereby decreasing natural capital, what is its net contribution to sustainable development? There is no easy answer to that question of course, but thinking about actions in this way can lead to changes in the planning and design stage, which can avoid negative impacts and increase the contribution of the initiative across the board.

Also, thinking about the environment as one sort of capital opens up questions about why we are prepared to diminish its capital stock, rather than live off the interest. We take risks with financial capital, sure, because the market place is designed to encourage and reward risk. But to do the same with the ecological systems that govern climate stability? Even the boldest financial investor would blanche at that sort of risk. And how come we recognise the flow of benefits to be had from investing in, say, our railway infrastructure, or education, yet don't do the same when it comes to the environment? Despite the evidence that even birdsong in airport business lounges and waterfalls outside hospital ward windows make us happier and stronger, we don't see investing in the environment as an important thing to do. Probably not out of badness, but certainly out of ignorance that without a healthy environment, there is no health, wealth and happiness for us.

As Daly and Cobb point out, the idea is not to overturn capitalism *à la* Karl Marx, but to modernise it in the light of new knowledge and understanding that was not available to people like Adam Smith living 230 years ago. In his foreword to the English edition of Daly and Cobb's *For the Common Good*, Paul Ekins sets out the central problem (Daly and Cobb, 1990). The models of conventional economics that have developed over the last couple of hundred years systematically marginalise and exclude two of humanity's most treasured assets: a supportive local community and a healthy, productive natural environment. They were regarded as either indestructible or not important.

One might imagine that if Adam Smith and James Hutton were miraculously to return to life now, they would not disagree with this point of view. Rather they would regret they did not do more to merge their theories at the time, and be surprised that it is taking us so long to put right what has, for many decades, been so obviously going wrong.

A research project carried out under the Economic and Social Research Council's (ESRC) Global Environment Change Programme by the Forum for the Future generated a tested set of 12 statements that would hold true if we were standing in a sustainable society. These statements themselves had to meet rigorous criteria: to be consistent; culturally neutral; non-prescriptive; congruent; and straightforward.

Table 11.3 12 Statements that would be true in a sustainable society

Financial Capital	1. Financial capital accurately represents the value of natural, human, social and manufactured capital.
Manufactured Capital	2. All infrastructure, technologies and processes make minimum use of natural resources and maximum use of human innovation and skills.
Social Capital	3. There are trusted and accessible systems of governance and justice. 4. Communities and society at large share key positive values and a sense of purpose. 5. The structures and institutions of society promote. stewardship of natural resources and development of people. 6. Homes, communities and society at large provide safe, supportive living and working environments.
Human Capital	7. At all ages, individuals enjoy a high standard of health. 8. Individuals are adept at relationships and social participation, and throughout life set and achieve high personal standards of development and learning. 9. There is access to varied and satisfying opportunities for work, personal creativity and recreation.
Natural Capital	10. In their extraction and use, substances taken from the earth do not exceed the environment's capacity to disperse, absorb, recycle or otherwise neutralise their harmful effects (to humans and/or the environment). 11. In their manufacture and use, artificial substances do not exceed the environment's capacity to disperse, absorb, recycle or otherwise neutralise their harmful effects (to humans and/or the environment). 12. The capacity of the environment to provide ecological system integrity, biological diversity and productivity is protected or enhanced.

It is encouraging that this approach allows policy-makers and communities to start with their own experience. Indeed, the sustainable capitalism logic is compatible with the many processes and systems which are developing and can be seen to add or derive value, for example the international standards ISO 14001 (Environment) and ISO 18001 (Health and Safety); the many Quality Management and Assurance schemes; Life Cycle Analysis; Industrial Ecology (see Graedel and Allenby, 1994, for example); Ecological Footprint (Worldwide Fund for Nature, 2005, for example); The Natural Step (see www.naturalstep.org); The Eco-Compass (Fussler and James, 1996); Mass Balance Analysis (Linstead and Ekins, 2001); Best Value (for local government in the UK, Scottish Executive, 2003, for example). All this should give encouragement for the journey to sustainability.

Then come the spanners in the works – or rather challenges. The physical challenge is embodied in the sheer size of many of the problems; for example, carbon dioxide emissions, waste accumulation, pollution and so on. Boiled down to the 'all important equation' first expressed in the 1970s (Holdren and Erlich, 1974) it can be expressed as

$$I = P \times C \times T$$

Where:
  I is Impact on the environment
  P is Population (number of people)
  C is Consumption of energy and materials (as manifest in the dominant economic growth indicator, gross national product)
  T is the techniques or technology of that consumption

The results of the equation depend on the population predictions (P) and different rates of growth assumed (C) (Ekins and Jacobs, 1995; Sadik, 1991). But the fundamental challenge to reducing the impact on the environment (I) arises from the need to vastly improve the efficiency of resource use through the technologies and techniques (T) to meet consumption and population requirements. The problem lies not in yet to be invented technologies, but in the politics and economics of change. For example, it is estimated that for each 1,000kg of 'stuff' consumed by an adult person living in a developed nation like Britain each year (about half of it food), another 10,000kg of 'stuff' has to be mobilised (see Schmidt-Bleek, 1992, for example). And while we pay across the counter for 1,000kg, the bill for the other 9,000kg (water, aggregate, waste, pollution and so on) is more often picked up by the environment or by other people, sometimes out of other budgets (health, for example), often in other countries. There is potential for huge efficiency gains.

Then there are the political challenges – here comes the real crunch given the relative lack of interest which many governments have in the environment, coupled with politicians' mass distrust of the not-for-profit sector. But we are witnessing some major changes and the key element of these, which is inspiring the growth of civil society activity, is people's concern for the environment and social justice – the very things that are usually excluded from governments' and businesses' definition of success. Robert Putman cites a decline in social capital as exemplified by a decrease in participation of Americans in institutions such as the church, political parties, school-parent associations and even ten-pin bowling league teams (Putnam, 2000).

This is in contrast to the view from The Johns Hopkins University Comparative Nonprofit Sector Project team. In their latest publication, Lester Salamon and his colleagues paint an alternative picture of what is happening in 'civil' society – a term used to distinguish people and communities from the state and the private business sector (Salamon et al., 2003). While there may well be a drop-off in some types of social engagement (such as bowling clubs) there is a boom in others. The Johns Hopkins team looked at the scope, structure, financing and role of civil society in a total of 35 countries, including the US and the UK, to conclude that 'in addition to its social and political importance the civil society sector turns out to be a considerable economic force' (Salamon et al., 2003). We should not be surprised, particularly since we see a growing disillusionment of people with their governments, an increase in social enterprises and a decrease in percentage of total shareholding by individuals (National Statistics, 2004).

The economic challenge is complex and requires re-examining at national and global levels. Constraints on the Smith-inspired notion of capitalism have become more evident not only as human population has risen in absolute numbers but also as the demand placed on environmental resources and services between rich and poor has rocketed disproportionately. Limited though it is, the OECD, for example, has begun to reframe the idea of a *New Economy* (OECD, 2003). The environment or natural capital do not figure in this new analysis of economic growth – so far. And beating strongly at its heart is still the central role of financial capital and the yet to be realised technological opportunities, such as biological, nano, and information and communication technologies. But firmly on the OECD scene as an essential actor on the economic stage is human capital, in particular the importance of investment in education.

Other examples of how social and manufactured capital are entering the widening definition of capital can be found in more progressive organisations and governments than the collective view provided by the OECD. For example, few governments any longer deny that investing properly in vibrant, attractive and well connected local communities is linked to reducing crime, ill health and other things that enter the cost side of the national accounts. Or that enjoying the benefits of a rail network that is on time, comfortable and safe depends on investment in the stock of infrastructure (rails, trains and so on) on which that service depends.

New approaches to measuring welfare in the broader sense are now showing that the prime indicator of economic success (gross domestic product) is little linked to well-being. Organisations like the New Economics Foundation have built on the start made by Daly and Cobb in the US to develop a UK Index of Sustainable Economic Welfare (ISEW). GDP is recalculated after adjustment for things like income inequality, unpaid domestic labour, environmental degradation, depletion of natural resources, long term environmental damages and so on. Figure 11.1 shows the resulting trajectory for per capita ISEW as against per capita GDP. The ISEW index is much closer to what people feel to be true about their lives, than are the Treasury indicators.

Figure 11.1 UK Index of Sustainable Economic Welfare and GDP per capita 1950–1996

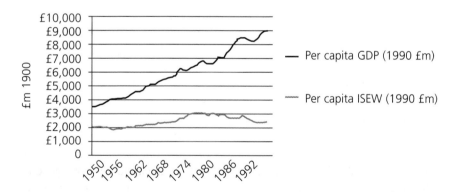

Source: Donovan et al., 2002

Finally there is the spiritual challenge. Here we need to address the dichotomy of thinking that exists between the things we feel are inherently sustainable and the mainstream of current unsustainable practice. We are *part of* the environment not *apart* from it.

The desired and required change of course to sustainable capitalism can be likened to that of a battleground where there needs to be strategic moves on four key fronts. It has not been possible here to detail further the arguments for the necessary four pre-emptive strikes in this decade's 'to do' list but they are given here as a guide to future discussion and action. First to build biological mass at all levels – back gardens to global eco-regeneration projects through investing in the supply side of environmental services; second to redefine security and start diplomacy from a sharing of common ground, environmental justice and vulnerability of environmental security; third to shape future markets and change the rules of the economy; and finally 'reknitting' social fabric by recreating communities through greater involvement of people and investing in social capital.

And then there is the lifelong learning component. We understand that the link between learning and behavioural change and engaging people in sustainability is a long-term investment but one which has to be started now. This is the beginning of the UN Decade of Education for Sustainable Development. The underpinning vision for the Decade is a world where everyone has the opportunity to benefit from education for societal transformation (CEC, IUCN, 2005).

It is clear that the outcomes of such a decade will be measured in new attitudes and values that guide better decisions, and actions that will put humankind on the path to sustainable development. This needs envisioning, critical and reflective thinking, participation from all stakeholders and systemic decision-making from a citizenry with the fundamentals of sustainability literacy.

We do have a great advantage in that a new, refreshing purpose for the human species is being articulated. Yes, it is the business of survival, as is evolutionarily usual. But by providing the missing connection between the two world views of Adam Smith and James Hutton it is possible to see how that survival can have a quality that adds to the sum of human happiness. Most importantly, we now have a pretty good idea of how to get there: by making top quality relationships with each other and with the environment the central objective of our economic system – *sustainable capitalism*. Just like the moral philosophers of a couple of hundred years ago, those advocating sustainable development as a new world view can provide both inspiration and practical solutions.

'The way we think influences what we see' (Sterling, 2004).

List of Hot Topics

Papers published to August 2005
http://www.obs-pascal.com/hottopics.php

1. **Jim Cavaye** *Social Capital: a Commentary on Issues, Understanding and Measurement*
   This paper explores what we know about social capital and what issues and questions remain. It is a commentary, raising issues and questions and seeking to stimulate debate.
   http://www.obs-pascal.com/resources/mowbray_dec_2004.pdf

2. **Ron Faris** *Lifelong Learning, Social Capital and Place Management in Learning Communities and Regions: A Rubik's Cube or a Kaleidoscope?*
   This paper links the work that has been done internationally on developing learning regions and learning communities, with the ways in which lifelong learning can enhance and extend social capital for individuals and groups.
   http://www.obs-pascal.com/resources/faris_2004.pdf

3. **Martin Mowbray** *Beyond Community Capacity Building: The Effect of Government on Social Capital*
   The distinctive contribution of this paper is its strong emphasis not only on locating the concept of social capital in the local or community context, but also in calling attention to the comprehensive framework of macro-economic and political forces and public policies which shape local interactions and networks, with very real implications for economic and social outcomes. In the author's view, both dimensions are necessary for adequate framing of the forces and social characteristics which we are trying to comprehend.
   http://www.obs-pascal.com/resources/mowbray_dec_2004.pdf

4. **Donna McDonald, Alison St.Clair Baker & Robert Hardy**
   Kent: A Virtual City Region
   This paper tells the unfinished story of growth and regeneration in the county of Kent in south east England and how Kent County Council is responding to the needs of its residents in aiming to create connected and sustainable communities, communities with a heart.
   http://www.obs-pascal.com/resources/kent_january2005.pdf

5. **Sara Parkin** *Sustainable Development*
   This hot topic paper is something of a special insight into what is perhaps the single most fundamental policy area facing the world in the twenty-first century.
   http://www.obs-pascal.com/resources/saraparkinapril2005.pdf

6. **Tom Healy** *Social Capital and Educational Policy: Serious Issues from an Imaginary Conversation with a Minister*
   Tom Healy's paper poses the deceptively simple question: if social capital is such a good idea, what can we do to build it? He offers differing takes on the relevance of social capital to public policy and provides an iterative analysis of the relationship between theory and practice.
   http://www.obs-pascal.com/resources/tomhealy_may2005.pdf

7. **Shirley Walters** *'Learning Cape' Aspirations: The Idea of a Learning Region and the use of Indicators in a Middle Income Country*
   The Western Cape Province in South Africa aspires to being a learning province, called the Learning Cape. The case study locates developments historically, describes competing under-standings of the Learning Cape, and analyses two strategies, which are illustrative of attempts to engage seriously with the concept.
   http://www.obs-pascal.com/resources/shirleywalters_june2005.pdf

8. **Markku Sotarauta** *Resilient City-Regions – Mission Impossible? Tales from Finland and Beyond about how to Build Self-Renewing Capacity*
   In this paper, Markku Sotarauta writes about his own and other cities that have attempted self-renewal (from rust belt blight to knowledge society regeneration), in order to ask what it is that gives a city-region the capacity for continuing self-renewal.
   http://www.obs-pascal.com/resources/markkusotarautaaugust2005.pdf

References

Abbott, J. and Ryan, T. (2000) *The Unfinished Revolution*. Stafford: Network Educational Press.

Alcock, P. (2004) 'Participation or pathology: contradictory tensions in area-based policy', *Social Policy and Society*, 3(2): 87–96.

Allen, P.M. (1990) 'Why the future is not what it was', *Futures*, 22(6): 555–570.

Asheim, B. and Dunford, M. (1997) 'Regional futures', *Regional Studies*, 31(5): 445–455.

Australian Bureau of Statistics (ABS) (2004) *Measuring Social Capital: An Australian framework and indicators*. Information Paper. Canberra: Australian Bureau of Statistics.

Balatti, J. and Falk, I. (2001) *Socioeconomic Contributions of Adult Learning to Community: A Social Capital Perspective*. Paper for the conference Wider Benefits of Learning: Understanding and monitoring the consequences of adult learning, European Society for Research on the Education of Adults (ESREA), 13–16 September, Lisbon, Portugal, CRLRA Discussion Paper, Launceston: University of Tasmania.

Barnett, R. and Griffin, A. (1997) *The End of Knowledge in Higher Education*. Cassell: London.

Bathelt, H., Malmberg, A. and Maskell, P. (2004) 'Clusters and knowledge: local buzz, global pipelines and the process of knowledge creation', *Progress in Human Geography*, 28: 31–56.

Belanger, P. (1994) 'Lifelong learning: the dialectics of 'lifelong Educations'', *International Review of Education*, 41: 353–381.

Benn, R. (1996) 'Access for adults to higher education: targeting of self-selection?', Journal of Access Studies, 11(2): 165–76.

Berry, J.M., Portney, K.E. and Thomson, K. (1993) *The Rebirth of Urban Democracy*. Washington: Brookings Institution.

Blacher, Y. (2003) 'Secretary's foreword', in Department for Victorian Communities, *Annual Report, 2002–2003*, p. 4. Melbourne: Department for Victorian Communities.

BMG (2002) *Kent County Council: Best Value Performance Indicators*.

Boateng, P. (2005) *Looking Back...Looking Forward* - Letter to Sir Sandy Bruce-Lockhart OBE, 28 February. London: HM Treasury.

Boschma, R. (2005) *Some Reflections on Regional Innovation Policy*. Paper prepared for the Expert Group meeting on 'Constructing Regional Advantage', Brussels, December 7, 2004, unpublished.

Bourdieu, P. and Passeron, J.C. (1977) *Reproduction in Education, Society and Culture*. London: Sage.

Bourdieu, P. (1980) 'Le capital social: notes provisoires', *Actes de la Recherche en Sciences Sociales*, 31: 2–3.

Braczyk, H-J., Cooke, P. and Heidenreich, M. (1998) *Regional Innovation Systems: The Role of Governances in a Globalized World*. London: UCL Press.

British Columbia (1974) *Towards the learning community*. Report of the Task Force on the Community College in British Columbia. Research and Development Division, Victoria: Department of Education.

British Columbia (1992) *Lifelong Learning for the 21st Century*. Victoria: Ministry of Education.

Brown, B. (2002) 'Cultivating hope and imagination', *Journal of Future Studies,* August.

Bullen, P. and Onyx, J. (1998) *Measuring Social Capital in Five Communities in NSW: An Analysis*. Centre for Australian Community Organisations and Management Working Paper Series No 41, University of Technology, Sydney.

Burns, G. (1998) *Toward a Redefinition of Formal and Informal Learning: Education and the Aboriginal People*. Presented at the joint session of New Approaches to Lifelong Learning (NALL) Conference and the Canadian Association for the Study of Adult Education (CASAE), University of Ottawa.

Butters, I., Lockie, S. and Fenner, M. (2003) *Kent County Council: Whole Life Cost Comparison Study: Six Schools in Kent*. London: Faithful and Gould.

Camagni, R. (1991) *Innovation Networks: Spatial Perspectives*. London: Belhaven Press.

Campbell, M., Devins, D., Foy, S., Hutchinson, J. and Walton, F. (1999) *Higher Education and Regional and Local Economic Development*. Council for Industry and Higher Education: London.

Canada (1991) *Learning Well...Living Well*. Consultation Paper of the Prosperity Secretariat. Ottawa: Ministry of Supply and Services.

Canada (1998) *Caring Canadians, Involved Canadians*. Highlights from the 1997 National Survey of Giving, Volunteering and Participating, Ottawa: Ministry of Industry.

Canada (1999) Speech from the Throne to Open the Second Session of the Thirty-Sixth Parliament of Canada, Ottawa: Prime Minister's Office.

Capra, F. (1982) *The Turning Point*. London: Wildwood House.

Capra, F. (1996) *The Web of Life: A New Scientific Understanding of Living Systems*. London: HarperCollins.

Capra, F. (2002) *The Hidden Connections: Integrating the Biological, Cognitive, and Social Dimensions of Life into a Science of Sustainability*. New York: Doubleday.

Carson, W.G. (2004) 'Is communalism dead? Reflections on the present and future practice of crime prevention', *Australian and New Zealand Journal of Criminology*, 37(1): 1–21.

Cavaye, J. (2004) *Social Capital: A Commentary on Issues, Understanding and Measurement*. Melbourne: Observatory Pascal – Place Management, Social Capital and Learning Regions.

CEC (2003) *The Role of the Universities in the Europe of Knowledge* COM(2003) 58 final.

Charles, D. and Benneworth, P. (2001) *The Regional Mission: The Regional Contribution of Higher Education: National Report*. London: Universities UK/HEFCE (published with nine regional reports).

Charles, D. and Benneworth, P. (2002) *Benchmarking Tool for HEI regional Engagement*. Bristol: HEFCE.

Charles, D. and Conway, C. (2002) *Higher Education Business Interaction Survey*. Bristol: HEFCE.

Charpentier, B. (2003) 'Spinning a web of social connections', *Concord Monitor*, 14 December (online).

Christie, I. and Warburton D. (eds) (2001) *From Here to Sustainability: Politics in the Real World*. London: Earthscan.

Cloonan, M. (2004) 'A capital project? 'The New Deal for Musicians' in Scotland', *Studies in the Education of Adults*, 36(1): 40–56.

Coffield, F. (ed) (2000) *Differing Visions of a Learning Society: Research Findings Volume II*. Bristol: Policy Press.

Cohen, W.M. and Levinthal, D.A. (1990) 'Absorptive capacity: a new perspective on learning and innovation', *Administrative Science Quarterly*, 35 (1): 128–52.

Cohen, W.M. and Levinthal, D.A. (1994) 'Fortune favors the prepared firm', *Management Science*, 40(2): 227–251.

Coleman, J.S. (1988) 'Social capital in the creation of human capital', *American Journal of Sociology*, 94: 95–120.

Coleman, J.S. (1990) *Equality and Achievement in Education*. Boulder: Westview Press.

Coleman, J.S. (1994) *Foundations of Social Theory*. Cambridge: Belknap Press.

Coleman, J. S., Campbell, E.Q., Hobson, C.J., McPartland, J., Mood, A.M., Weinfeld, F. D., and York, R.L. (1966) *Equality of Educational Opportunity*. Washington: United States Government Printing Office.

Colley, H, Hodkinson, P. and Malcolm, J. (2002) *Non-Formal Learning: Mapping the Conceptual Terrain*. A Consultation Report. Leeds: University of Leeds Lifelong Learning Institute. Also available in the informal education archives: http://www.infed.org/archives/e-texts/colley_informal_learning.htm

Commission on Education and Communication (CEC), IUCN (2005) *Engaging People in Sustainability*. Gland, Switzerland: IUCN.

Commission of European Communities (2000) *A Memorandum on Lifelong Learning*. Commission Staff Working Paper, Brussels.

Committee on Higher Education (1963) *Higher Education*, Cmnd. 2154 (Robbins Report). London: HMSO.

Cooke, P. (2002) *Knowledge Economies: Clusters, Learning and Cooperative Advantage*. London: Routledge.

Costello, P. (2003a) *Is Faith a Lost Cause?* Address to Anglicare lunch, 27 June.

Costello, P. (2003b) *Building social capital*. Address to the Sydney Institute, 16 July.

Cox, E. (1995) *A Truly Civil Society: 1995 Boyer Lectures*. Sydney: ABC Books.

Cox, E. and Caldwell, P. (2000) 'Making policy social', in I. Winter (ed.) *Social Capital and Public Policy in Australia*, pp. 43–73. Melbourne: Australian Institute of Family Studies.

Craig, G. (2002) 'Towards the measurement of empowerment: the evaluation of community development', *Journal of the Community Development Society*, 33: 124–46.

Cullen, M. and Whiteford, H. (2001) *The Interrelationships of Social Capital with Health and Mental Health*. Discussion Paper. Canberra: Commonwealth Department of Health and Aged Care.

Daly, H.E. and Cobb, J.B., Jr. (1990) *For the Common Good: Redirecting the Economy toward Community, the Environment and a Sustainable Future*, London: Greenprint.

Daniel, J., Habib, A. and Southall, R. (2003) *The State of the Nation: South Africa 2003–2004*. Cape Town: HSRC Press.

Dave, R.H. (1973) 'On learning strategies for lifelong education' in R.H. Dave (ed), *Reflections on Lifelong Education and the School*, UIE monograph 3, pp. 43–58. Hamburg: Unesco Institute for Education.

Defra (2005a) *One Future – Different Paths. The UK's Shared Framework for Sustainable Development*. London: HMSO.

Defra (2005b) *Securing the Future – Delivering UK Sustainable Development Strategy*. London: HMSO.

Delahunty, M. (2003) Minister for Women's Affairs, Speech to International Women's Day Lunch, Melbourne, 7 March. http://www.dvc.vic.gov.au/speeches/2003_Womens_Day_Lunch_speech.doc

Delanty, G. (2002) 'The university and modernity: a history of the present', in Robins, K. and Webster, F. (eds), *The Virtual University: Knowledge,*

Markets and Management. Oxford: OUP.

Department of Education and Science (1973) *Adult Education: A Plan for Development* (The Russell Report). London: HMSO.

DfEE (1999) *Practice, Progress and Value: Assessing the Value of Learning Communities*. Prepared by NIACE and the University of Birmingham for the Learning City Network.

DfES (2003) *Every Child Matters*. Green Paper. London: HMSO.

DfH (2004) *Choosing Health: Making Healthy Choices Easier*. CM6374. London: Department for Health.

Dika, S.L. and Singh, K. (2002) 'Applications of social capital in educational literature: a critical synthesis', *Review of Educational Research*, 72(1): 31–60.

Division for Lifelong Learning (2001) *Developing the Learning Cape: Occasional Paper*. Cape Town: University of Western Cape.

DLL/ODA (2005) *Towards Developing and Implementing Lifelong Learning Policy: Indicators for a Learning Cape*. Draft report for Department of Economic Development. Cape Town: PAWC.

Donovan N., Halpern, D. and Sargeant, D. (2002) *Life Satisfaction: The State of Knowledge and Implications for Government*. London: Strategy Unit, UK Cabinet Office. http://www.wcfia.harvard.edu/conferences/socialcapital/Happiness%20Readings/DonovanHalpern.pdf

Dryzeck, J.S. (1993) 'Policy analysis and planning: from science to argument', in: F. Fischer and J. Forester (eds). *The Argumentative Turn in Policy Analysis and Planning*. Albany: UCL Press.

Duke, C. (2002) *Lifelong Learning in the 21st Century University*. Melbourne: Royal Melbourne Institute of Technology University. http://www.ala.asn.au/research

Duke, C. (2004) *Learning Communities. Signposts from International Experience*. Leicester: NIACE.

Easterlin, R.A. (2001) 'Income and happiness: towards a unified theory', *Economic Journal*, 111: 465–484.

Edvinsson, L. and Malone, M.S. (1997) *Intellectual Capital*. New York: Harper Collins.

Edwards, B and Foley, M.W. (1997) 'Social capital and the political economy of our discontent', *American Behavioural Scientist*, 40(5): 669–78.

Ekins, P., Hillman, M. and Hutchinson, R. (1992) *Wealth beyond Measure: An Atlas of New Economics*. London: Gaia Books.

Ekins, P. and Jacobs, M. (1995) 'Environmental sustainability and the growth of GDP: conditions of compatibility', in V. Bhaskar and A. Glyn (eds). *The North, the South and the Environment*. London: Earthscan.

Elsdon, K.T., Reynolds, J. and Stewart, S. (1995) *Voluntary Organisations: Citizenship, Learning and Change*. Leicester: NIACE.

Etzioni, A. (1994) *The Spirit of Community: The Reinvention of American Society*. New York: Simon & Schuster.

Etzkowitz, H. (2004) 'The evolution of the entrepreneurial university', *International Journal of Technology and Globalisation*, 1: 64–77.

European Commission (2001) *Making a European Area of Lifelong Learning a Reality*. Brussels: Communication from the Commission.

European Commission (2002) *Call for Proposals (EAC/41/02) European Networks to Promote the Local and Regional Dimension of Lifelong Learning (The "R3L" Initiative)*. Brussels: Commission of the European Communities.

Falk, I. and Kilpatrick, S. (1999) *Refocusing on Learning Regions: Education Training, and Lifelong Learning for Australia's Well Being*. Centre for Research and Learning in Regional Australia. Hobart: University of Tasmania.

Faris, R. (2001) *The Way Forward: Building a Learning Nation Community by Community*. Discussion paper prepared for the Walter and Duncan Gordon Foundation, Toronto. http://members.shaw.ca/rfaris/LC.htm

Faris, R. and Peterson, W. (2000) *Learning-Based Community Development: Lessons Learned for British Columbia*. Victoria: Ministry of Community Development, Cooperatives and Volunteers.
http://members.shaw.ca/rfaris/LC.htm

Farr, J. (2004) 'Social capital: a conceptual history', *Political Theory*, 32(1): 6–33.

Feinstein, L., Hammond, C., Woods, L., Preston, J. and Bynner, J. (2003) *The Contribution of Adult Learning to Health and Social Capital*. London: Centre for Research on the Wider Benefits of Learning, Institute of Education.

Field, J. (2000) *Lifelong Learning and the New Educational Order*. Stoke on Trent: Trentham Books.

Field, J. (2001) 'Lifelong Education', *International Journal of Lifelong Education*, 20: 3–15.

Field, J. (2003a) *Social Capital*. London: Routledge.

Field, J. (2003b) 'Social capital and lifelong learning: survey findings on the relationship between sociability and participation', in N. Sargant and F. Aldridge (eds), *Adult Learning and Social Division: A Persistent Pattern*, pp. 32–41. Leicester: NIACE.

Field, J. (2005) *Social Capital and Lifelong Learning*. Bristol: Policy Press.

Fine, B. (2001) *Social Capital versus Social Theory: Political Economy and Social Science at the Turn of the Millennium*. New York: Routledge.

Flier, B., Van Den Bosch, F. and Volberda, H.W. (2003) 'Co-evolution in strategic renewal behaviour of British, Dutch and French financial incumbetents: interaction of environmental selection, institutional effects and managerial intentionality', *Journal of Management Studies*, 40(8): 2163–2186.

Flora, C.B. and Flora, J.L. (1993) 'Entrepreneurial social infrastructure: a necessary ingredient', *Annals of the American Academy of Political and Social Sciences*, 539: 48–58.

Florida, R. (1995) 'Towards the learning region', *Futures*, 27(5): 527–536.

Florida, R. (2002) *The Rise of the Creative Class and how it's Transforming Work, Leisure, Community and Everyday Life*. New York: Perseus Books Group.

Freire, P. (1973) *Pedagogy of the Oppressed*. Harmondsworth: Penguin Books.

Frey, B.S. and Stutzer, A. (2002) *Happiness and Economics: How the Economy and Institutions Affect Human Well-Being*. New Jersey: Princeton University Press.

Fukuyama, F. (1999) 'The great disruption: human nature and the reconstitution of social order', *The Atlantic Monthly*, May.

Fussler, C. and James, P. (1996) *Driving Eco-Innovation: A Breakthrough Discipline for Innovation and Sustainability*. London: Pitman Publishing.

Galston, W. (1996) 'Unsolved mysteries: the Tocqueville fives II', *The*

American Prospect, 26(May-June): 20–25. http://epn.org/prospect.org/print-friendly/print/V726/26-cnt1.html.

Garlick, S. (2000) *Engaging Universities and Regions: Knowledge Contribution to Regional Economic Development in Australia*, Evaluations and Investigations Programme (00/15), Department of Education, Training and Youth Affairs, Commonwealth of Australia.

Georgescu-Roegen, N. (1971) *The Entropy Law and the Economic Process*. Cambridge, MA: Harvard University Press.

Gibbons, M., Limoges, C., Nowotny, H., Schwatzman, S., Scott, P. and Trow, M. (1994). *The New Production of Knowledge*. London: Sage.

Giddens, A. (1999) Arnold Goodman Charity Lecture, 15 June. http://www.cafonline.org/goodman/go_speech99.cfm.

Gil, D.G. (1992) *Unravelling Social Policy: Theory, Analysis, and Political Action Towards Social Equality*, 5th edn. Rochester: Schenkman Books.

Gilbert, A. (1987) 'Forms and effectiveness of community participation in squatter settlements', *Regional Development Dialogue*, 8: 56–85.

Goddard, J., Charles, D., Pike, A., Potts, G. and Bradley, D. (1994) *Universities and Communities*. London: Committee of Vice-Chancellors and Principals.

Goddard, J.B. and Chatterton, P. (1999) *The Response of Higher Education Institutions to Regional Needs*. Paris: OECD.

Golding, B. (2004) *The Applicability of Networks to Australian Adult and Vocational Learning Research*. School of Education, University of Ballarat. Paper given at seventh Australian VET Research Association Conference. http://www.avetra.org.au/Conference_Archives/2004/documents/PA046Golding.PDF

Gorard, S. and Rees, G. (2002) *Creating a Learning Society? Learning Careers and Policies for Lifelong Learning*. Bristol: Policy Press.

Graedel, T.E. and Allenby, B.R. (1994) *Industrial Ecology*. Englewood Cliffs, NJ: Prentice Hall.

Granovetter, M. (1973) 'The strength of weak ties', *American Journal of Sociology*, 78(6): 1360–80.

Grattan, M. (2003) 'Costello, the social capitalist', *The Age*, 22 June.

Grenier, P. and Wright, K. (2003) *Social Capital in Britain: An Update and*

Critique of Hall's Analysis. International Working Paper No.14, Centre for Civil Society, LSE.

Haig-Brown, C. (2000) *Taking Down the Walls: Communities and Educational Research in Canada's 21st Century.* NALL Working Paper #17 –2000, The Dr. Reginald B. Moase Invitational Address delivered to the 19th Annual Graduate Student Conference-Faculty of Education, St. Catherines Ontario, September 23, 2000.

Harriss, J. (2002) *Depoliticizing Development: The World Bank and Social Capital.* London, Anthem Press.

Hatton, M. (ed) (1997) *Lifelong Learning: Policies, Practices and Programs* (an APEC publication). Toronto: Humber College.

Hawe P. and Shiell, A. (2000) 'Social capital and health promotion: a review', *Social Science and Medicine,* 51(6): 871–85.

Healey, P., Madanapour, A. and Magalhaes, C. (1999) 'Institutional capacity-building, urban planning and urban regeneration projects' in M. Sotarauta (ed), *Urban Futures: A Loss of Shadows in the Flowing Places? Futura,* 18(3): 117–37.

Healy, T. (2005) *In Each Other's Shadow: What has been the Impact of Human and Social Capital on Life Satisfaction in Ireland?* Unpublished PhD Thesis, UCD.

Hedoux, C. (1982) 'Des publics et des non-publics de la formation d'adults', *Revue française de Sociologie,* 23: 253–74.

Heilbroner R. (1983) *The Worldly Philosophers.* Harmondsworth: Penguin.

Hertz, N. (2001) *The Silent Takeover: Global Capitalism and the Death of Democracy.* London: Heinemann.

Himmelstrup, P. (1981) 'Introduction', in P. Himmelstrip, J. Robinson and D. Fielden (eds), *Strategies for Lifelong Learning: A Symposium of Views from Europe and the USA,* pp. 11–23. Esberg: University Centre of South Jutland and the Association for Recurrent Education, UK.

HEFCE (2004) *Student volunteering: case studies of good practice from HEACF: Projects funded by the Higher Education Active Community Fund; case studies compiled by the Careers Research and Advisory Centre. HEFCE Good Practice report 2004/21.* Bristol: HEFCE.

HMG (2004a) *Housing Act.* London: HMSO.

HMG (2004b) *Planning & Compulsory Purchase Act*. London: HMSO.

Holdren, J. and Erlich, P. (1974) 'Human population and the global environment', *American Scientist*, 62(May-June): 282–92.

Holland, J. (1998) *Emergence: From Chaos to Order*. Cambridge, MA: Perseus books.

Hollnsteiner, M.R. (1979) 'Mobilizing the rural poor through community organization', *Philippine Studies,* 27: 387–416.

Horin, A. (2003) 'A politician and his trusty old platitudes', *Sydney Morning Herald*, 19 July.

HSRC (2003) *Human Resource Development Review 2003: Education, Employment and Skills in South Africa.* Cape Town: HSRC Press.

Hutton, J. (1795) *Theory of the Earth with Proofs and Illustrations*. Vol 1, Edinburgh.

Jackson, T. (1996) *Material Concerns: Pollution, Profit and Quality of Life.* London: Routledge.

Johnson, D., Headey, B. and Jensen, B. (2003) *Communities, Social Capital and Public Policy: Literature Review.* Institute of Applied Economic and Social Research, University of Melbourne, Working Paper, 26/03 November 2003.

Johnson, S. (2002) *Emergence: The Connected Lives of Ants, Brains, Cities, and Software*. New York: Simon and Schuster.

Kash, D.E. and Rycroft, R. (2002) 'Emerging patterns of complex technological innovation', *Technological Forecasting and Social Change,* 69: 581–606.

Kautonen, M., Kolehmainen, J. and Koski, P. (2002) *Yritysten innovaatioympäristö: Tutkimus yritysten innovaatiotoiminnasta ja alueellisesta innovaatiopolitiikasta Pirkanmaalla ja Keski-Suomessa.* [Innovation environment of firms: a study on innovation activity of firms and regional innovation policy.] TEKES, Teknologiakatsaus 120/2002. Helsinki.

Kawachi, I., Kennedy, B.P. and Lochner, K. (1997) 'Long live community: social capital as public health', *American Prospect*, 35: 56–59. http://www.inequality.org/roseto.html.

KCC (2003) *What Price Growth?* Maidstone: Kent County Council.

Keating, D. and Hertzman. C. (1999) *Developmental Health and the Wealth of Nations*. New York: Guildford Press.

Kent and Medway Economic Board (2002) *Strategic Economic Framework for Kent and Medway* (under revision with full revision available spring 2006 - available at http://www.kmeb.org.uk/pdfs/kmeb_framework.pdf).

Kent Association of Local Authorities (2000) *Kent Design: A Guide to Sustainable Development*. Kent: KALA.

Kent Partnership (2002) *Vision for Kent: Kent People in Partnership for a Better Tomorrow*. Maidstone: Kent County Council.

Kent Thameside Delivery Board (2005) *Kent Thameside Regeneration Framework*.

Kidd, J.R. (1978) 'Organizing for lifelong learning', in J. R. Kidd and G. R. Selman (eds), *Coming of Age: Canadian Adult Education in the 1960s*, pp. 78–85. Toronto: Canadian Association for Adult Education.

Kidd, J. R. (1980) 'A nation of learners', in P.M. Cunningham and I. Larson (eds), *Yearbook of Adult and Continuing Education 1980–81*, pp. 2–13. Chicago: Marquis Academic Media.

Kim, L. and Nelson, R.R. (2000) (eds) *Technology, Learning and Innovation: Experiences of Newly Industrializing Economies*. Cambridge: Cambridge University Press.

Kostiainen, J. and Sotarauta, M. (2003) 'Great leap or long march to knowledge economy: institutions, actors and resources in the development of Tampere, Finland', *European Planning Studies,* 10(5): 415–38.

Lambert, R. (2003) *The Lambert Review of Business-University Collaboration*. London: HMSO.

Lauglo, J. (2000) 'Social capital trumping class and cultural capital? Engagement with school among immigrant youth', in S. Szreter, J. Field and T. Schuller (eds), *Social Capital: critical perspectives*, pp. 142–67. Oxford: Oxford University Press.

Leadbeater, C. (2003) *The Man in the Caravan and Other Stories*. London: IDeA.

Lengrand, P. (1970) *An Introduction to Lifelong Education*. Paris: Unesco.

Leopold, A. (1949) *A Sand County Almanac and Sketches Here and There*. New York: Oxford University Press.

Lester, R.K. and Piore, M.J. (2004) *Innovation – The Missing Dimension.* Cambridge: Harvard University Press.

Lin, N. (1988) 'Social resources and social mobility: a structural theory of status attainment', in: R. Breiger (ed), *Social Mobility and Social Structure.* Cambridge: Cambridge University Press.

Lindeman, E. (1961) *The Meaning of Adult Education.* Montreal: Harvest House.

Linstead, C. and Ekins, P. (2001) *Mass Balance UK: Mapping UK Resource and Material Flows.* London: Forum for the Future.

Livingston, D. (2000) *Exploring the Icebergs of Adult Learning: Findings of the First Canadian Survey of Informal Learning Practices.* Working paper, Research Network on New Approaches to Lifelong Learning. Toronto: OISE.

Lovelock, J. (1979) *Gaia: A New Look at Life on Earth.* Oxford: Oxford University Press.

Lundvall, B-Å. and Borrás, S. (1997) *The Globalising Learning Economy: Implications for Innovation Policy.* Luxembourg: Office for Official publications of the European Communities.

Lundvall, B-Å. and Johnson, B. (1994) 'The learning economy', *Journal of Industry Studies,* 1(2): 23–42.

MacNeil, T. (2001) *Lifelong Learning as a Public Policy in Canada.* An unpublished paper prepared with the support of the Canadian Alliance of Education and Training Organizations (CAETO), Ottawa.

March, J. (1991) 'Exploration and exploitation in organizational learning', *Organization Science*, 2(1): 71–87.

Maskell, P. (1996) *Learning in the Village Economy of Denmark. The Role of Institutions and Policy in Sustaining Competitiveness.* Danish Research Unit on Industrial Dynamics (DRUID), Working Paper No. 96–6.

Maskell, P. (2000) 'Social capital, innovation and competitiveness', in S. Baron, J. Field and T. Schuller (eds), *Social Capital: critical perspectives*, pp. 111–23. Oxford: Oxford University Press.

Martinez-Vela, C. and Viljamaa, K. (2004) *Becoming High-Tech: The Reinvention of the Mechanical Engineering Industry in Tampere, Finland.* MIT IPC Local Innovation Systems Working Paper 04–001.

Mayer, M. (2003) 'The onward sweep of social capital: causes and consequences for understanding cities, communities and urban movements', *International Journal of Urban and Regional Research,* 27: 110–32.

McDowell, G. (2001) *Land Grant Universities and Extension into the 21st Century: Negotiating or Abandoning a Social Contract.* Ames: Iowa State University Press.

Mckelvey, B. (1999) 'Complexity theory in organization science: seizing the promise or becoming a fad', *Emergence: A Journal of Complexity Issues in Organizations and Management*, 1: 5–32.

McMurray, J. (2003) 'Costello v Latham: whose social capital is bigger?', *Crikey*, 5 August.
http://www.crikey.com.au/politics/2003/08/05–socialcapital.print.html.

Milbrath, L. (1996) 'Envisioning a sustainable society', in R. Slaughter (ed). *New Thinking in a New Millennium.* Routledge: London.

Mizstal, B. (2000) *Informality: Social Theory and Contemporary Practice.* London: Routledge.

Moodie, R. (2003) Speech launching the 'Together we do better campaign', 2 April 2003.
http://www.togetherwedobetter.vic.gov.au/news/viewNews.asp?newsID=22.

Morgan, K. (1997) 'The learning region: institutions, innovation and regional renewal', *Regional Studies*, 31: 491–503.

Morris, M. (2004) 'Wonder: Piers Gough's public toilet, Westbourne Grove, London', *The Guardian,* 24 November.

Mowbray, M. (2004a) *Beyond Community Capacity Building: The Effect of Government on Social Capital.* Melbourne: Observatory Pascal – Place Management, Social Capital and Learning Regions. http://www.obs-pascal.com/resources/mowbray2004.pdf.

Mowbray, M. (2004b) 'The new communitarianism: building great communities or brigadoonery?' *Just Policy*, 32: 11–20.

Muntaner, C. and Lynch, J. (2002) 'Social capital, class gender and race conflict, and population health: an essay review of *Bowling Alone*'s implications for social epidemiology', *International Journal of Epidemiology*, 31: 261–7.

Mustard, F. and Keating, D. (1993) *The National Forum on Family Security – Social Economic Factors and Human Development.* Toronto: The Canadian Institute for Advanced Research.

National Statistics (2004) *Share Ownership: A Report on Ownership of Shares as at 31st December 2003*. London: Office of National Statistics. http://www.statistics.gov.uk/downloads/theme_economy/ShareOwnership2003.pdf

Natrass, B. and Altomare, M. (1999) *The Natural Step for Business: Wealth, Ecology, and the Evolutionary Corporation*. Gabriola Island: New Society Publishers.

Navarro, V. (2002) 'A critique of social capital', *International Journal of Health Services*, 32(3): 423–32. http://www.fhi.se/pdf/Critiqueofsocialcpital.pdf.

NCIHE (1997) *Higher Education in the Learning Society, Chapter 12: The Local and Regional Role of Higher Education*. London: HMSO.

NLGN and IDeA (2003) *Improvement and the Use of Local Public Service Agreements – Lessons from Kent and Middlesborough*. London: NLGN.

Nonaka, I. and Konno, N. (1998) 'The concept of 'ba': building a foundation for knowledge creation', *California Management Review*, 40(3): 40–54.

Nooteboom, B. (2000) *Learning and Innovation in Organizations and Economies*. New York: Oxford University Press.

ODPM (2002) *Quality and Choice: A Decent Home for All*. London: ODPM.

ODPM (2003) *Sustainable Communities: Building for the Future*. London: ODPM.

ODPM (2004a) *The Egan Review: Skills for Sustainable Communities*. London: ODPM.

ODPM (2004b) *The Future of Local Government: Developing a 10 Year Vision*. London: ODPM.

ODPM (2005) *Delivering Sustainable Communities Summit*. London: ODPM.

OECD (1973) *Recurrent Education: A Strategy for Lifelong Learning*. Paris: OECD.

OECD (1996) *Lifelong Learning for All*. Paris: OECD.

OECD (2001a) *Cities and Regions in the New Learning Economy*. Paris: OECD.

OECD (2001b) *The Well-being of Nations: The Role of Human and Social Capital*. Paris: OECD.

OECD (2003) *The Sources of Economic Growth in OECD countries*. Paris: OECD

O'Hara, K. (2004) *Trust: From Socrates to Spin*. Cambridge: Icon Books.

Parcel, T. and Menaghan, E.G. (1994) 'Early parental work, family social capital and early childhood outcomes', *American Journal of Sociology*, 99(4): 972–1009.

Parkin, S. (2000a) 'Sustainable development: the concept and the practical challenge', *Civil Engineering*, 138(November): 3–8.

Parkin, S. (2000b) 'Contexts and drivers for operationalizing sustainable development', *Civil Engineering*, 138(November): 9–15.

PASCAL (2003) *Observatory PASCAL* (information brochure). http://www.obs-pascal.com. Melbourne: PASCAL.

PAWC (2001) *Preparing the Western Cape for the Knowledge Economy of the 21st Century* (White Paper). Cape Town: PAWC.

PAWC (2003) *Final Report: A framework for developing a Human Resources & Skills Development Strategy in the Western Cape*. Cape Town: PAWC.

Perry, S.E. (1987) *Communities on the Way: Rebuilding Local Economies in the United States and Canada*. Albany: State University of New York Press.

Pike, B. (2003) *Community Building – It's Good for our Towns and Suburbs, but is it Really Good for our Health?* Our Community and Catholic Social Services Conference, Melbourne, 8 April.

Piven, F.F. and Cloward, R.A. (1979) *Poor People's Movements: Why They Succeed, How They Fail*. New York: Vintage Books.

Plowman, I., Ashkanasy, N., Gardner, J. and Letts, M. (2003) *Innovation in Rural Queensland: Why Some Towns Thrive while Others Languish*. An unpublished report on research undertaken by UQ Business School, University of Queensland and Queensland Department of Primary Industries.

Pollitt, K. (1996) 'For whom the ball rolls', *The Nation*, 15 April. http://www-personal.umich.edu/~skassner/Eng125Pollitt.html.

Porter, M. E. (2000) 'Location, competition and economic development: local clusters in a global economy', *Economic Development Quarterly*, 14(1): 15–34.

Portes, A. (1998) 'Social capital: its origins and applications in modern sociology', *Annual Review of Sociology*, 24: 1–24.

Preston, J. (2004) *Identity, Learning and Engagement: A Qualitative Inquiry using the NCDS*. Wider Benefits of Learning Research Report No. 13. London: Institute of Education.

Productivity Commission. (2003) *Social Capital: Reviewing the Concept and its Policy Implications*. Research Paper. Canberra: AusInfo.

Provincial Department of Social Services and Poverty Alleviation (2005) *Social Cluster, Social Capital Formation Document*, Cabinet Legkotla. Cape Town: PAWC.

Putnam, R.D. (1993a) 'The prosperous community: social capital and public life', *The American Prospect,* Spring: 35–42.

Putnam, R.D. (1993b) *Making Democracy Work: Civic Traditions in Modern Italy*. Princeton: Princeton University Press.

Putnam, R. (1994) 'What makes democracy work?', *IPA Review*, 47(1): 31–34.

Putnam, R. (1995) 'Bowling alone: America's declining social capital', *Journal of Democracy,* 6(1): 65–78.

Putnam, R. (2000) *Bowling Alone: The Collapse and Revival of American Community*. New York: Simon and Schuster.

Putnam, R. (2001) 'Social capital measurement and consequences', *Isuma*, 2(1): 41–51. http://www.isuma.net/v02n01/putnam/putnam_e.shtml

Putnam, R. and Feldstein, L.M with Cohen, D. (2003) *Better Together: Restoring the American Community*. New York: Simon and Schuster.

Readings, B. (1996) *The University in Ruins*. Cambridge: Harvard University Press.

Reay, D., David, M. and Ball, S. (2005) *Degrees of Choice: Social Class, Race and Gender in Higher Education*. Stoke-on-Trent: Trentham Books.

Reed, P. (2000) *Developing Civic Indicators and Community Accounting in Canada*. Ottawa: Statistics Canada / Carleton University.

Rogers, B. (2003) 'The chicken soup of the social sciences', article in *Prospect* reproduced in *Amitai Etzioni Notes*, 5 November.

Rosenfield, S.A. (2002) *Just Clusters: Economic Development Strategies that Reach More People and Places*. Carrboro, North Carolina: Regional Technology Strategies.

Ross, D. and Shillington, R. (1990) *Economic Dimensions of Volunteer Work in Canada*. Ottawa: Secretary of State.

Rubenson, K. (2001) *Lifelong Learning for All: Challenges and Limitations of Public Policy*. The Swedish Ministry of Education and Science European Conference: Adult Lifelong Learning in a Europe of Knowledge, Eskilstuna, March 23–25.

Sadik, N. (1991) *The State of the World Population*. New York: UNFPA.

Safford, S. (2004) *Searching for Silicon Valley in the rust belt: the evolution of knowledge networks in Akron and Rochester*. MIT IPC Local Innovation Systems Working Paper 04–002.

Salamon, L.M., Wojciech Sokolowski, S. and List, R. (2003) *Global Civil Society: An Overview*. Baltimore: John Hopkins University.

Salvaris, M., Burke, T., Pidgeon, J., and Kelman, S. (2000) *Social Benchmarks for Victoria*. Consultants Report for the Department of Premier and Cabinet, Victoria.

Sankey, K. and Osborne, M. (2005) 'Lifelong learning reaching regions where other learning doesn't reach', in R. Edwards et al. (eds), Researching Learning Outside the Academy. London: Routledge (in press)

Saskatchewan. (1972) *Report of the Minister's Advisory Committee on Community Colleges*. Regina: Department of Continuing Education.

Saskatchewan. (1973) *The Saskmedia Report*. Regina: Department of Continuing Education.

Schmid, A.A. and Robison, L.J. (1995) 'Applications of social capital theory', *Journal of Agriculture and Applied Economics* 27(1): 59–66.

Schmidt-Bleek, F. (1992) 'MIPS - a universal ecological measure', *Fresenius Environmental Bulletin*, 1: 306–11.

Schuller, T. (1998) *Discussion on Social Capital The Learning Age: Towards a Europe of Knowledge*. Conference Report, Manchester, p.196.

Schuurman, F.J. (2003) 'Social capital: the politico-emancipatory potential of a disputed concept', *Third World Quarterly*, 24(6): 991–1010.

Scottish Executive (2003) *Local Government in Scotland Act 2003*. Edinburgh: HMSO.

Senge, P., Cambron-McCabe, N., Lucas, T., Smith, B., Dutton, J. and Kleiner, A. (2000) *Schools That Learn*. London: Nicholas Brealey.

Serageldin, I. and Steer, A. (1994) 'Expanding the capital stock', in I. Seregeldin and A. Steer (eds). *Making Development Sustainable: From Concepts to Action*, ESD Occasional Paper Series No 2. Washington DC: The World Bank.

Siisiäinen, M. (2000) *Two concepts of social capital: Bourdieu vs Putnam.* Paper presented at ISTR Fourth International Conference, The third sector: For what and for whom? Dublin, 5–8 July.

Singer, P. (2004) *The President of Good and Evil: The Ethics of George W. Bush.* New York: Dutton.

Skocpol, T. (1996) 'Unravelling from above', *The American Prospect*, 25: 20–25 http://epn.org/prospect/25/25-cnt2.html.

Sotarauta, M. (1996) *Kohti epäselvyyden hallintaa: Pehmeä strategia 2000–luvun alun suunnittelun lähtökohtana* [Towards management of ambiguity: soft strategy as a point of departure of policy-making in the beginning of 21st century]. Acta Futura Fennica, 6. Jyväskylä: Finnpublishers.

Sotarauta, M. (2005) 'Shared leadership and dynamic capabilities in regional development', in I. Sagan and H. Halkier (eds). *Regionalism Contested: Institution, Society and Territorial Governance.* Cornwall: Ashgate.

Sotarauta, M. and Bruun, H. (eds) (2002) *Nordic Perspectives on Process-Based Regional Development Policy.* Nordregio report 2002:3. Stockholm.

Sotarauta, M. and Srinivas, S. (2005) *The Co-Evolution of Policy and Economic Development: A Discussion on Innovative Regions.* MIT IPC Local Innovation Systems Working Paper 05–001.

Sotarauta, M. and Srinivas, S. (forthcoming 2006) 'Co-evolutionary policy processes: understanding innovative economies and future resilience', *Futures.*

Sousa, J. and Quarter, J. (2003) *Informal and Non-formal learning in Non-profit Organizations.* Working paper, Research Network on New Approaches to Lifelong Learning. Toronto: OISE.

Srinivas, S. and Viljamaa, K. (2003). *BioTurku: 'newly' innovative? The rise of bio-pharmaceuticals and the biotech concentration in southwest Finland.* MIT IPC Local Innovation Systems Working Paper 03–001.

Statistics South Africa (2001) *Census 2001.*

St Clair, R. (2005) 'Do capital-based perspectives help to conceptualise the potential of lifelong learning?', in P. Coare, P. Armstrong, M. Boice and L.

Morrice (eds), Diversity and Difference in Lifelong Learning, pp. 355–62. Brighton: SCUTREA.

Sterling, S. (2004) *LinkingThinking: Unit 1 Education and Learning, an introduction.* Perthshire: WWF Scotland.

Stewart-Weeks, M. (1998) *Place Management: Fad or Future?* An address to an open forum of the Institute of Public Administration, NSW Division. August.

Stewart-Weeks, M. (2000) *Place Management: Governance in the Network Society.* A keynote paper to a conference convened by Families, Youth and Community Care Queensland.

Storper, M. (1995) 'The resurgence of regional economies, ten years later: the region as a nexus of untraded interdependencies', *European Urban and Regional Studies*, 2(3): 191–221.

Strathdee, R. (2005) *Social Exclusion and the Remaking of Social Networks.* Aldershot: Ashgate.

Szreter, S. (1999) *New Political Economy for New Labour: The Importance of Social Capital.* Political Economy Research Centre Policy Papers – Paper 15, Sheffield: University of Sheffield.

Szreter, S. (2000) 'Social capital, the economy, and education in historical perspective', in S. Baron, J. Field and T. Schuller (eds), *Social Capital: Critical Perspectives*, pp. 56–77. New York: Oxford University Press.

Szreter, S. and Woolcock, M. (2002) *Health by Association? Social Capital, Social Theory and the Political Economy of Public Health.* Von Hügel Institute Working Paper, WP 2002–13, December.

Tarrow, S. (1996) 'Making social science work across space and time: a reflection on Robert Putnam's *Making Democracy Work*', *American Political Science Review*, 90(2): 389–97.

Thomas, A. (1963a) 'The adult student: his role as student and member', in J. Kidd (ed), *Learning and Society*, pp.318–27. Toronto: Canadian Association for Adult Education.

Thomas, A. (1963b) 'The learning society', in J. Kidd (ed), *Learning and Society*, pp.405–10. Toronto: Canadian Association for Adult Education.

Thomas, A. (1987) 'Government and adult learning', in F. Cassidy and R. Faris (eds) *Choosing Our Future: Adult Education and Public Policy in Canada.* Toronto: OISE Press.

Thompson, E.P. (1970) *Warwick University Ltd.* Harmondsworth: Penguin.

Thurow, L. (2000) *Building Wealth: The New Rules for Individuals, Companies, and Nations in a Knowledge-Based Economy.* New York: Harper Business.

Torres, R.M. (2003) 'Lifelong learning: a new momentum and a new opportunity for adult basic learning and education in the South', *Adult Education and Development,* S60: 239.

Tuijnman, A. and Boudard, E. (2001) *International Adult Literacy Survey: Adult Education Participation in North America: International Perspectives.* Ottawa: Statistics Canada.

UKPIU (United Kingdom Performance and Innovation Unit) (2002) *Social Capital: A Discussion Paper.* April.

Unesco (1972) *Learning to Be: The World of Education Today and Tomorrow* (The Faure Report). Paris: Unesco.

Unesco (1996) *Learning: The Treasure Within* (The Delors Report). Paris: Unesco.

United Kingdom (1919) *Report of the Adult Education Committee of the UK Ministry of Reconstruction.* London: HMSO.

United Nations Development Programme (UNDP) (1999) *UNDP Human Development Report 1999: Globalization with a Human Face,* Oxford and New York: Oxford University Press.

USDHUD (2000) *Colleges and Communities: Gateway to the American Dream. The State of the Community Outreach Partnership Centres Program, 2000,* Washington: HUD.

Vuorensyrjä, M. (2001) 'Tacit Human Capital', in E. Pantzar, R. Savolainen and P. Tynjälä (eds), *In Search for a Human-Centred Information Society,* pp. 57–79. Tampere: Tampere University Press.

Walters, S. (2005a) 'Learning region', in L. English (ed.). *International Encyclopedia of Adult Education,* pp. 360–2. New York: Palgrave MacMillan.

Walters, S. (2005b) 'Learning society and knowledge society in South African debates. A literature review', in M. Kuhn and R. Sultana (eds). *The Learning Society in Europe and Beyond.* Bern: Peter Lang.

Walters, S. and Etkind, R. (2004) *Developing a Learning Region: What can Learning Festivals Contribute?* Paper presented at the AERC Conference, Victoria, Canada.

Wanless, D. (2002) *Securing our Future Health: Taking a Long-Term View*. London: HM Treasury.

Western Cape Provincial Development Council (2004) *The Framework Agreement for Growth and Development and Social Dialogue*. Cape Town: Provincial Development Council.

Western Cape Provincial Treasury (2003) *Western Cape Socio-Economic Review 2003*. Cape Town: PAWC.

Western Cape Provincial Treasury (2005) *Western Cape Provincial Economic Review and Outlook 2005*. Cape Town: PAWC.

Whiteley, P. F. (2000) 'Economic growth and social capital', *Political Studies*, 48(3): 443–66.

Williams, R. (1975) *The Country and the City*. St Albans: Paladin.

Woolcock, G., Renton, D. and Cavaye, J. (2004) *What Makes Communities Tick? Local Government and Social Capital Action Research Project*. Brisbane: Local Government Association of Queensland.

Woolcock, M. (1999) *Social Capital: The State of the Notion*. Paper presented at a multidisciplinary seminar on Social Capital: Global and Local Perspectives, Helsinki, April 15.

World Commission on Environment and Development (1987) *Our Common Future*. Oxford: Oxford University Press.

Worldwide Fund for Nature (2005) *Europe 2005: The Ecological Footprint*. Godalming: WWF.

Wotherspoon, T. and Butler, J. (1999) *Informal Learning: Cultural Experiences and Entrepreneurship Among Aboriginal People*. NALL Working Paper #04–1999

Yeaxlee, B. (1929) Lifelong Education. London: Cassell.

Zappala, G. and Green, V. (2001) *Addressing Disadvantage through Place Management: Is There a Role for Nonprofit Organizations?* Working Paper No. 3, Research and Social Policy Team, The Smith Family.

Index

Index